God B----

Steve Kowalski

Pastor Albert Howard Sr.

To

PASTORING

From

PIMPING

To

PASTORING

From

PIMPING

A 30 Plus Year Journey from Street Life to Grace

Based on a True Story

BISHOP ALBERT HOWARD, SR.

FIRST EDITION.

Editing, Interior Layout and Cover Design by Colleen R. Carpenter, Word Processing Diva.com.

ISBN-13:
978-1499191943

ISBN-10:
1499191944

ACKNOWLEDGMENTS

I would like to start this book by acknowledging a few people, some of whom are still here and others have gone on. The first name would be Patricia Dillard, my first prostitute, a young lady who had come out of New York City to visit her brother in Cleveland. We were introduced and later began a relationship. Patricia and I started out as girlfriend and boyfriend, but eventually became pimp and prostitute. She was later murdered.

I could never write a book without acknowledging just a few of my friends who were also murdered in those mean streets of Cleveland, Ohio:

Erving Lowe
Steve Perkins
Benny Taylor
Freddie Tate

The devil desired to kill me also, but God said no. God said Pimping Al you are not to die, but live, and declare my truth.

Psalm 118-17:

I shall not die, but live and declare the works of the Lord.

DEDICATION

This book is dedicated to the lost souls who need to know that Jesus is a Savior.

Psalm – 40:2 – *"He brought me up also out of an horrible pit, out of the miry clay, and set my feet upon a rock, and established my goings."*

CONTENTS

"God didn't promise days without pain, laughter without sorrow, or sun without rain, but He did promise strength for the day, comfort for the tears, and light for the way. If God brings you to it, He will bring you through it."

– unknown

INTRODUCTION

It is my hope in writing this book that it will touch lost souls in the world today. I was one of them. I lived the street life for 30 plus years, but God's grace found me and gave me a new life. I am no longer lost, but have found the peace and joy that only a personal relationship with Christ can bring. I wrote this book because I want to give back some of the things that I have received. For anyone reading this book who may be downtrodden and in despair, or feel they have no way out, it is my desire to impart some kind of hope.

This book will show you that God has the power to stop a drug dealer from dealing drugs or stop a pimp from pimping. To readers who feel they're on a downward road, for those who may be at a crossroad in life and don't know which way to turn, this book is living proof that change is possible. God's grace can take them through.

Perhaps some young man will read this book and have a change of opinion about living the street life. So many people who were in that lifestyle when I was there are no longer here to write a book or to tell the story, but God spared my life and allowed me to live through difficult times.

When I set out to write this book, God placed a lady in my life to help me with it. I had total confidence in Ms. Carpenter. She was real about it all. There were times when she would look at me and say, "Pastor Howard, I want this book to be the best it can be, but most of all I want it to touch people's lives, maybe the life of a young man who may be headed in the wrong direction. Some young lady out there may need guidance about a decision. There may be something in this book that will encourage them to turn their lives around."

These days I go to God for everything and I trust him for everything. I'm just grateful and thankful that he placed someone in my life to help me with this book.

If just one person decides to turn their life around after reading this book and gives their life to Christ, then it will be well worth it. As a Pastor, my greatest desire is for souls to be saved. If just one soul is saved by the writing of this book then my heart will be made glad.

"For we are His workmanship, created in Christ Jesus for good works, which God prepared beforehand so that we would walk in them."

– Ephesians 2:10

Chapter 1

THE EARLY DAYS

My story began on November 9, 1945. I was born in Alabama and brought to Cleveland, Ohio as a baby. God gave me two loving parents. Lula Mae Vincent Howard was my mother and a perfect picture of love. Most of the children in our neighborhood loved her, because she opened her doors and her heart to everyone.

My father was Mann Howard, but most people called him Sam, even my sister, brother and me. We never called him daddy. I have an older sister, Beatrice, who had a different mother. She called him daddy. My mother loved Beatrice just as she loved us and we were raised to love one another. We didn't know anything about half-sister or half-brother in our home. I had great respect for my father. He taught me how to be a man and will always be my hero.

My childhood was a happy one, but one day all hell broke loose. When I was 12 years-old, my mother and father separated. I had always been very good in school and got good grades, but when my dad left it was all downhill for me. I would sit in the classroom looking up at the ceiling, hoping my dad would come back home. He never did, and my whole life began to change.

I have a younger sister, Laura, and younger brother, James who were left there with me in this situation. I can remember so clearly my mother looking me in the face and saying, "Albert, you are the man of the house. Look out for your little brother and sister." That's when I began to learn how to be responsible.

My mother and father never owned their own home, and with my father being out of the house my mother had to take a day job to help ends meet. I learned how to clean the house and look out for Laura and James to help my mother, because when she came home from work she would be so tired. My mother only earned five dollars a day plus a bus ticket doing day work. My father had become an alcoholic and would come by from time to time to check on us.

We were so poor, always moving from one neighborhood to another. Because we moved so frequently and were always meeting new children, I had to learn how to fight.

My mind had become too occupied to study any school work and I lost interest in school. My grades began to drop and my mind turned to girls. Girls were on my mind all the time. In those days I had been told that my hair was long, my smile was alright and my conversation was out of sight! At age 16, I dropped out of the school I was attending which was Central High on 40th Street, between Central and Cedar. I was living on East 39th Street, between Quincey and Central Avenue. Back in those days people made fun of that neighborhood. They called it the "Dirty Thirties."

Chapter 2

A TASTE OF PIMPING

When I was growing up, most of the beautiful white women I ever saw were the ones on our 3-channel television. Back then I remember watching actresses like Jane Mansfield, Marilyn Monroe and Elizabeth Taylor. I was inspired and motivated, but as a young Black man I'd see those fine white women on television with their long hair, but I lived next door to a Black woman who had hair like my sister.

I decided one day that I would have a white woman for myself. My dad who was raised in the south, grew up afraid of the white man's law. He was afraid that if you got caught with a white woman you'd be hung from a tree. I told my dad, "Listen, I respect what you're saying, but I don't have any fear. I'm not afraid of the white man or his rope."

At the age of 16, I was fortunate enough to meet not just any white woman, but a rich white woman who once laid $65,000 in my hands because she cared so much about me. Her name was Olga, and she lived in a town called Beachwood.

I can remember it like it was yesterday. Olga and I met at a party. My cousin, Robert Goodgame, knew one of Olga's friends. The friend invited Olga to the party and Robert invited me. Olga was a beautiful Italian woman with a gorgeous figure. I never really knew how old she was, but I did know that she was a lot older than me. When I met Olga she didn't work, nor did she need to. Her husband owned several businesses so she was very well situated financially.

Although Olga's husband had Black people working for him, he didn't really like Blacks and often referred to them as "niggers." He did his best to discourage Olga from spending time with them. One day he hired a Black man to clear snow from the driveway at their home. Over time Olga got to know the man and found him to be a kind person. She realized that Black people weren't always what her husband made them out to be.

When we were introduced at the party, Olga could see that I was much younger in age than anyone she would normally be attracted to, but I was an outgoing and outspoken person so I started asking Olga for dances. We were having a good time and started talking as we danced. She told me that I was too young for her, but I persisted and finally encouraged Olga to give me her telephone number.

About a week later I called the number and we talked on the phone for a while. I asked Olga if she would meet me somewhere so we could talk some more. She said, "Sure. Why not." We met at a Chinese restaurant back in Cleveland on 79th and Cedar. We sat down and had dinner together. From that point on we became very good friends. Olga saw something in me that made her want to provide me with some of the finer things in life. Anything I wanted she bought it, and after a while Olga fell in love with me.

Olga had several cars including a new Oldsmobile and new Cadillac. She would often allow me to drive her Cadillac and we would cruise around town just enjoying each other's company. Here I was, just 16 years of age, driving through the neighborhood in a Cadillac with a beautiful Italian woman who was at least twice my age. Other men in the neighborhood would look on with envy wishing they could replace me in the seat of that car sitting next to Olga. The older men in the neighborhood would cheer me on by saying, "Boy, you is a Pimp!" At the time, I didn't even know what a pimp was, but I later learned what a "real" pimp was.

My father worried about the fact that I was spending time with a white woman and driving her Cadillac. The only thing he could see in his mind was that the white man was going to stop the car one night, pull me out of there, put a rope around my neck and hang me from a tree. I had no fear about seeing Olga and my mind was made up. This was what I wanted and it was what I was going to do.

I didn't know it then, but as my life began to unfold and I look back over the years, that was truly when my pimping began. I was a 16 year-old, good-looking Black man, who had drawn the attention of a rich, beautiful white woman.

I was still living at home when Olga took me out of my mother's house and provided me with my own apartment. Even though she was a married woman, she would come down and spend as much time with me as she could. Olga paid the rent and everything else. She made sure all of my needs were met. She got my hair done, bought my clothes, and saw to it that I always had spending money. It was a beautiful feeling.

Chapter 3

THE GOOD GIRL

I had a friend who was older than I was named Willie Christian. For the most part I liked to hang out with older people, because I felt people my age didn't understand the things I did. Willie had a beautiful wife named Beatrice and they would open their doors and make everyone feel welcome. Willie also had a sister named Honey who lived in the unit upstairs from him. We hardly saw Honey because her husband was a very jealous man. I thank God for the Christian family.

One day we were out on the porch and I was putting some waves in Willie's hair. I had to learn how to do a lot of things back then and I had to learn fast. I looked out into the yard and saw this young girl walking by. From what I could see, she had a nice looking face and a very nicely built body. I had never seen her before, nor had she seen me.

By this time I'd had lots of experience with older women and younger woman too. My confidence about them was so high that I believed if there was any woman I wanted, I had what it took to get them. I hollered down to the girl walking by and simply said to her, without even knowing her name, "I'm going to get you!" She looked up with big beautiful eyes and said "No you are not." I took off running and caught up to her. I found out her name was Mary Ann Turney and we became friends. Mary was attending East High School and I started going up there to walk her home.

I met Mary Ann's mother, whose name was also Mary, who later became like a mother to me. Mary Ann had come from a family where her mother and father had also separated. Her mother was a hard working woman who loved her children like my mother loved us. I don't believe Mary's mother allowed her to receive company at that time, but here I come, Mr. Nice Guy. When I wanted something or someone I knew how to put on my best side. Her mother would let me come over and take her daughter to the library. What her mother didn't know was that we never went to the library.

One day, after all the lies about the library, Mary had to tell her mother the heartbreaking news that she was pregnant! Mary was so ashamed and embarrassed, but she had to tell her mother. Her mother's response was that Mary was too young to have a baby and needed to have an abortion. Mary had such love for her unborn child that she convinced her mother to let her keep the baby. She suffered a stroke during the pregnancy and her face became twisted, but God gave her favor and straightened out her face. Mary prayed that God would allow her to be at least 16 years-old when our firstborn arrived. Her prayer was answered because on May 16th, Mary turned 16 years-old, and on June 9, 1964, God blessed us with Dwight, our beautiful son.

Chapter 4

NEW WIFE, NEW LIFE

My mother and father tried talking me into marrying Mary because they felt it was the right thing to do, but if the truth be told I didn't feel that way, nor did Mary or her mother. I still had two ladies in my life, Gwen and Delores, and I believe Mary still had Walter and Ike on her mind. We didn't really know each other like that.

When Mary told me that she was pregnant a second time, our parents thought for sure that we should be married so at 19 years of age, on April 21, 1965, I married Mary. I know now for sure that love had nothing to do with it. We got on welfare and stayed there for a big part of our marriage, until finally she began to say things to me about not being a "real man."

I went out to look for work and the only job I could find, without a high school diploma, was a Bus Boy at the Brown Derby for 75 cents an hour or a dish washing job for $1.25 per hour. I remember times when I would wash so many dishes until I would dream about dishes.

Mary had two uncles who were older than me and had more street smarts than I did. There were four brothers, but these two, Willie and Frank, had their hands into just about everything you could imagine. They had whore houses, an after-hour house, a store and other businesses. They loved their niece Mary, and when they found out it was me she was pregnant by, man they really lost it. They didn't want their niece to be with me in any kind of way. They told Mary's mother, "This nigger got more women than Carter got pills!"

There were many times when I would go to their store and get food and money to make ends meet for the rest of the month. One day I went to her uncle Willie to borrow some money and he said to me, "Ain't you tired of asking me and Frank to borrow money? You have lots of girlfriends. Why don't you learn how to ask them for some money?"

At the time, my friend Patricia Dillard was working a regular job, and every Friday when she got paid she would take me to the House of Style on Crawford Road, right off Hough Avenue. Chris Wright was the proprietor and Master Barber. He was indeed a master at styling and cutting men's hair and was well known in Cleveland for his expertise. It was a beautiful thing just to go to the barber shop. Not only was Chris my barber, he also became a father-figure to me and some of the other guys who would come there like Desembly, Frank, Little John, Big John, Big Tim and many others.

I took Willie's advice about asking my "girlfriends" for money, and I never had to ask men for money ever again. I started pimping out of Willie and Frank's whore house located on Hough Avenue. I started out with one lady, Patricia Dillard, but soon and very soon I had a stable of women. One day Willie and I had a falling out and he said to me, "Get your whores and get out!" I did just that and never brought another lady to work out of Willie's house ever again. I moved on and learned the game. Because I was true to the game, the game was true to me.

Believe it or not, I was able to stay in the game for 30 years. Most folks in Cleveland may remember me by several names: "Pimping Al," "Big Al," "Prince Al," and "P.P.A.," which stood for "Pretty Pimping Al." My ladies worked between 82nd and 84th and Hough Avenue, near the Fleet

Wing Gas Station. The Astor Theater was on the corner of 84th and Hough.

You may wonder where my wife was during this time. We were together, sometimes. When she found out what I was doing she would run back home to her mother, but after a few days to a week she would call me and I would let her come back home.

During one of the times Mary had run off I stopped by my mother's house on Wade Park. I met a lady there named Dorothy who was 13 years my senior. She would come to visit her daughter who lived downstairs beneath my mother. I was 21 years-old at the time and had been pimping for two years. On several occasions while visiting my mother, if I was sitting near the window I would see Dorothy coming by to see her daughter. She would try to rush off without having a conversation, but I finally got her to warm up to me and we became very close.

I can truly say that Dorothy was the woman who taught me how to treat a lady! She had three daughters whom she loved more than me or her husband Danny. We saw each other for awhile, but she eventually told me to go back home to my wife. Dorothy and I lost contact for over 40 years, but somehow God allowed us to find each other before she passed away. I thank God for her daughter Sandy who helped make it possible until the end.

Chapter 5

THE BIRTH OF PIMPING AL

I went back to my wife and tried all over again. I believe it's safe to say that Mary had lost any feelings that she might have had for me. I think both of us were trying to hang in there for the children's sake, but I had allowed the streets to change me. I no longer felt like Albert. I felt more like "Pimping Al."

My mother and father's first reaction when they realized I was pimping was that they were upset and disappointed. My mother took it the hardest because she had great hopes for my future. She felt like I could have been something more and would always say I could have done better. My brother and sister weren't happy about my pimping either.

When people see the pimping lifestyle they imagine many things, but the truth of the matter is that it became my lifestyle because I was attracted to the lights and glamour. I didn't live in the best neighborhood growing up and I always wanted more, something better. Back in those days, men that I admired were the ones who appeared to have nice things in their lives. They were willing to go out and try to make something happen.

I knew that one day I would get away from my old neighborhood. I remember seeing men drive around in beautiful cars, dressed in nice suits. I learned that Black men in those days, the 50s and 60s, didn't have many business opportunities available to them. For those fortunate enough to have a business, it usually consisted of a pool room or bar.

I think back to my cousins, the Goodgame brothers, who played an important role in my life. They were older than I was and more like big brothers. They set good examples for me, one of which was having a strong work ethic. They all had 9-5 jobs. Willie worked for the International Salt Company back in Cleveland. He brought job applications home for me to fill out, but I never did.

Willie's older brother Roy worked for Premier Manufacturing Company, also in

Cleveland. He got me a job with him, but I may have lasted a week before I walked out. Their other brother, Robert was a welder. I went to school and took up that trade. I learned how to weld and received my blueprint ratings. I stayed on the job for a few weeks and quit.

Another cousin, William Pierce, worked for the Alward Construction Company in Bernardsville, New Jersey. He and his wife Betsy Mae invited my wife and me to come to New Jersey so I could pursue a job in construction. Mary and I decided we would leave the children back in Cleveland with her mother for a while and come to New Jersey. This was hard for me because I had several ladies working at the time. The pimping was good, but I had to make a choice. I wanted to keep pimping because of the money, but I loved my wife and children so I decided to make a change. New Jersey seemed to be a good move because it would have been hard for me to stay in Cleveland and not be a pimp.

I had a stable of ladies working for me when I had to tell them that I was leaving and going to New Jersey to get a job. They didn't want me to go but I had my mind made up. I wanted to hold my family together. I loved my family and they needed financial security. Up to that point, I just hadn't educated myself well enough to get the type of job that I needed to support them.

19

Other pimps I knew just couldn't understand how I could make such a move and they would often joke about it. Prostitutes leaving pimps was a common thing, but to hear about a pimp leaving his prostitutes was something that rarely came up. This wasn't the only time I left my prostitutes, because I actually did it twice. I left them back then and I again bowed out when I decided to change my life.

I stayed true to my decision, gave up pimping and Mary Ann and I moved to New Jersey. We were going to find jobs, settle in, and come back to Cleveland to get the children. Things seemed to be going just as we had planned. I got the construction job and my cousin, Ethel Goodgame, got my wife a job at a watch company in Parsippany, New Jersey.

After about three weeks of being in New Jersey, things began to fall apart. My wife and I started missing the children and we missed being in Cleveland. Mary decided one day to go to work and not come back. She took a Greyhound bus to Paramus and temporarily took a live-in job. She called her mother and told her that she would soon be returning home. Mary finally called me to let me know where she was. I went and picked her up and we both returned to Cleveland.

Patricia, my first prostitute, had continued working the strip while I was away and was giving my cousin Christine money to put away for me. When I returned to Cleveland Chris said, "I've saved this money that Patricia asked me to put up for you." She went to her bedroom and reached under the mattress pulling out a few hundred dollars which she gave to me. She had also put some money into a bank account, so in total I had about $1,300.00. I picked up where I left off.

My wife had very little understanding of the pimping part of my life and she really beat me down about it. I don't know if she truly realized the torture that she put me through, always comparing me to the man next door who had a "normal" job. She was always telling me what a great father figure he was to his children because he went to work and was home in the evenings. It was hard hearing those things from my wife, but I was determined that even though I didn't have the type of education I felt I needed, I was still going to make a way to provide for my wife and children.

I understand things better now than I did then. My wife wanted me to go to work, punch a clock and hold down a 9-5 like my cousins were doing. I'm thankful for them because they were all hard-working men, and so was my dad. I probably would have been a hard working man too, but it just wasn't in the cards for me.

I had taken those welding classes with the intention of getting a job at the shipyard. I actually became pretty good at it and was offered a job in Ohio, which I didn't take. When I think about it now, if I had gone to the shipyard and became a welder I would not have had the life experience that pimping afforded me to have.

The Goodgame brothers showed me that a man could get a job and do well, but that type of situation wasn't for Al. I just couldn't do it. I had to go out into the world and meet people, see things and go places. The 9-5 life wasn't for me.

When I think back to that time, I know that Mary and I were trying to stay in the marriage because of our children, but in the year 1970, Mary finally turned it loose and let go of our marriage. She divorced me and my pimping truly began. I was pimping in full force and not looking back!

As a pimp, I travelled all over the United States and met people from all walks of life. For me pimping was more than just an occupation, because anything a man does for 30 plus years is a career. Today I understand it better by and by. God had different plans for me, for this hour, for this day and time. My pimping career gave me important life experience. I learned about people, places and things so that today I can stand before God's people and declare the truth.

Chapter 6

PROSTITUTES – THE ART OF BUILDING & KEEPING A STABLE

I thank the lord for my family. I have strong bonds with them and always will because this was the way I was raised, to love your family. I believe that helped me even in the game. Coming from a loving family gave me lots of understanding during my years of pimping on how to bring my ladies together and have them interact as family.

The ladies who worked for me came from various backgrounds. Some of my prostitutes were college educated women, and some were even housewives looking to earn some extra cash. I always took good care of my ladies and they didn't have to want for anything. I bought them houses, cars, beautiful clothes and jewelry. Whatever they needed, Pimping Al took care of it. My ladies were also loyal and some stayed with me for 10 years or longer.

If you think about it, real men, regardless of what their occupation may be, like real women and that was my business. My business was women and I was blessed. I am so thankful to say that in over 30 years of being in the game and on top of the game, even though men and women were dying all around me, God did not suffer any of my prostitutes to ever lose their lives. That's a blessing right there.

I prayed that none of the prostitutes who worked for me would be murdered and today I can truly say that God answered that prayer. They've been robbed and sometimes beaten, but none was ever murdered, except for my first prostitute and that didn't happen while she was with me. She was murdered because she married a weak-minded square, who was too insecure to let her go when she wanted to leave him.

Some may wonder how I was able to spend so much time around beautiful women and not become sexually attracted or involved with them. All I can say is that my mind was not preoccupied with sex. I believed sex was mind over matter and my matter was money, so it was very easy for me to be around the women in my stable. We weren't in it for the sex act. We came into the game because of the glamour and money.

Prostitutes back then were very skilled at what they did because they treated it like a business. They had to make the johns understand that this was a "business deal." They would tell the men, "I'm not your girlfriend and I'm not your wife. Most importantly you need to know that I'm not in love with you. I'm rendering you a service and this is what it's going to cost you. This is what you can do, and this is what you cannot do."

There was always a potential for trouble in that line of work. When you go into a room, undress and lay down with someone you barely know, that's trouble right there. But a professional prostitute, a true prostitute, knows how to handle herself in most situations where she may have a problem with a john. All of that was part of the game.

For the most part, I didn't have to get involved with how the ladies handled the johns, but when you're dealing with money, wine and women there's always going to be some trouble. I remember so many fights because some of the johns would come in and spend a little bit of money, but they wanted a whole lot of service.

The johns would often get aggressive and try to take their money back, but when Pimping Al was on the scene none of that was going down. You were going to get the service you paid for, nothing extra. It didn't matter who you were, what size you were, or where you came from because I was man enough to deal with whatever situation came up that my ladies couldn't handle.

I didn't have a problem putting people in their place because my father always reminded me growing up, "Son, know your place and stay in it. If you know your place and stay in it then nobody will have to put you in it." I knew my place and my place was to stand up and be a man, and that's what I was going to do. The johns were going to know that I was a man and the police were going to know it as well.

It was my responsibility to hire prostitutes and there were times when it was necessary for me to fire them too. It wasn't hard for Pimping Al to fire prostitutes at all. I was running a business, and if a prostitute didn't comply with certain rules I had in place she was automatically fired.

A lady once asked me what I said to women to encourage them to turn to a lifestyle of prostitution. I thought about Patricia, my first prostitute. I knew that she had feelings for me and I had some for her. At first, I didn't know exactly what to say to encourage her to try prostitution so I decided I would show her.

Patricia would get paid from her regular job on Fridays, and on weekends she would do the things she could for me out of her paycheck. I would take her on the strip so she could see all of the ladies, how well they were dressed and how fast they were going in and out of the whore houses. I would say to her, "We could do the same thing. We could make money too."

As Patricia and I walked the strip, I pointed out the pimps riding by in their new cars and the way they were dressed. I finally got Patricia to understand that if she would do the same thing those prostitutes were doing, I could look like those pimps, drive a beautiful car and wear those fine clothes. These were things she wanted for me.

She kept her day job, but on the weekends Patricia would come down to the strip and prostitute her body. The money started coming in so well that Patricia decided to let go of her Monday to Friday job. What she earned during the week on her job, she could make in one night working as a prostitute. It was her feelings for me that caused her to want to do things for me.

Patricia was my first lady and she turned out to be a dedicated prostitute of mine for many years.

The only reason she left was because I had become so large in the game and had developed a stable of women. She had also been arrested so many times that she had developed quite a criminal record. To continue prostituting would mean jeopardizing her freedom.

Patricia wound up quitting prostitution and returning to Alabama. She got married, had a daughter and was working as a nurse. One day she decided she was going to leave her husband. He, not like myself, was unable to let her leave so he took a shotgun and took her life. It's unfortunate, but if you listen to the news or read your newspaper you will find that many women are murdered by weak, possessive men who don't have the strength to let go.

I learned as I grew in the game. I wouldn't just send ladies out I learned how to turn them out as well. I knew how to catch and keep a lady. I had prostitutes from all walks of life and from different nationalities. Pimps have different methods of turning out ladies, but for me it meant winning their confidence and getting them to care for me. I found that most prostitutes were looking for something because most women don't go out intentionally looking for a pimp. Some came from broken homes, or had run away from home. Others had abusive fathers, or were dealing with difficult situations. They came looking for love, a home or a father figure.

I would say to women today to be sure that you know what the game is all about, not just the glamour and the glitz, but be aware of the circumstances and situations beyond things that the eyes can see. So many prostitutes have lain down with a stranger to never get up again. Also, there are so many women marrying different men for different reasons. They are lying down with someone that they think is their friend for 5, 10 or even 20 years. At some point that woman may decide she wants to move on without him.

The difference between a husband and a pimp is that some married men get a notion in their minds that a wife is his forever and that's not always so. There are also weak-minded fellows who believe that if they can't have a woman, no one can. When a prostitute comes to a pimp, a real pimp knows that this prostitute came to pay, not to stay.

During my pimping days, white men didn't seem to have a problem with pimps who had Black prostitutes, but it was hard for them to see Black pimps with white prostitutes on the strip. Years ago police officers would arrest white prostitutes and take them to jail rather than see them on the strip giving a Black man their money. They just couldn't understand how they could give all their money to a pimp. Many police officers would arrest these ladies, but they never made it to the jail house. These women were often so beautiful and appealing, that some of those officers would stop between buildings or behind buildings and have sex with the prostitutes before releasing them.

I have many memories of the prostitutes who worked for me. I remember a time when I was chosen by a young lady named Regina. She was a number one prostitute. Regina had been across the country and had traveled all over the United States; she knew her business. She and I were out riding one night, listening to music and feeling good. She looked over and said to me, "Al, do you realize how big your pimping is here in Cleveland, Ohio? Your name is ringing. They're calling you the number one pimp. In other words you are an Ohio Player, but I think that your pimping is bigger than just Ohio. I think that maybe you should take your pimping across the country."

There were so many pimps in the game who never went any further than one neighborhood to another, and I was in that same place going from the Fifth District to the Third District. I looked at Regina and said, "You know, that's something to think about." Basically, the only reason I had not traveled across the country was because I wanted to stay close to my children and be there when they needed me.

After talking to Regina, I decided it was time to take my pimping to another level. Back then there was a place in Boston called the Sugar Shack. I was told folks from all over the country would meet there and have a wonderful time. I drove Regina to the Cleveland Hopkins Airport and put her on a plane to Boston. Three to four days later she called me and said, "Al, you need to come on up. The money is good and I'm doing very well. I've stacked up a great amount of cash for you that you'll have when you arrive in the city."

I took two of my prostitutes with me, one white and one Black. Back then white girls were called "Snow," and the Black girls were called "Coal." The ladies and I headed to Boston. When we arrived there the city was on fire. We checked into a downtown Howard Johnson's hotel near the Greyhound Bus Station. There were strips all over the place and girls were working everywhere. I was excited. After checking into the room, I showered, dressed up and headed for the Sugar Shack.

My friend, Slim Carter had arrived in town as well. He and I stood on the street corner just talking. I remember so well how Mr. Carter looked at me and said, "Al, fish are biting." Immediately I turned to look behind me and there was a beautiful Italian lady standing there smiling at me. I said to her, "Is there something you would like to say to me?" She said, "Yes there is." I asked her to speak on.

The woman said, "My girlfriend and I saw you earlier and I said to her, wow, look at that fine man standing there. I know he's a pimp and I would like to get to know him. I went on about my business because I knew that in order to get to know you I would need to have some money. I went on to work and made my money. At the end of the night I came back by where I had seen you earlier and there you were standing talking to another pimp. I just stood behind you because I know better than to interrupt pimps when they are conversating."

Finally I said to the woman, "Would you like to come with me?" She said, "I sure would." We went to my hotel and as we entered the room she started to undress. I said to her, "No. No. That's not the way I do it." I walked out onto the balcony and asked her to join me there so we could talk. She was looking at me with lust in her eyes, but I had money, not sex on my mind.

I asked her if she had traveled before or been across the country. She said, "No. I've just been here working in Boston but never across the country." I explained to her that I had come from Cleveland, Ohio and that my mind was set on traveling across the country, from the east coast to the west coast. I said to her, "It's a big world out there. Would you like to see some of it with me?" She said, "I surely would." I told her that the following day at check out time I would be leaving Boston and heading to Atlanta, Georgia. That would be my first stop. I had heard so many stories about the Atlanta underground and how pimps would be there on the strip on Peachtree Street.

The woman agreed to go with me to Atlanta and pulled out her money and gave it to me. When a woman chooses a pimp she pays her pimp. By her paying me she had become my "lady." She couldn't seem to stop looking at the bed in the hotel room, but again I told her no, I didn't do it like that. She looked at me and said, "Wow. That's different because a lot of pimps here in Boston will have sex with you without getting any money." I said to her, "I don't know how they pimp here in Boston, but I can tell you how I do it. I don't have sex with my ladies and I get my money upfront. That way if I get paid up front and you leave you don't owe me anything because I got my money in the beginning."

We established that fact right then and there. Don't even think about sex with me. I wanted your mind on money because that's what I needed. Sleeping with my prostitutes was something I just didn't do. That kind of situation could create jealousy and other issues between the women, which would definitely disrupt my cash.

The following day I checked out of the hotel and left Boston. I had four women in the car with me, two white and two Black. We traveled about 23 hours with me driving my custom built Cadillac, which had its own built in television and telephone. We were headed for Atlanta, Georgia, listening to music and enjoying ourselves.

We made several stops along the way and people would stop and ask if I would allow them to take pictures of my automobile. My 1974, candy apple red Cadillac was just that beautiful. The car had been built by Jerry Roman and had been entered into several automobile shows taking first place trophies. Today I still have that '74 Cadillac. I don't use it anymore, but keep it as a reminder of my past life and how things used to be.

When I drove down the street in that car it was something people hadn't seen before and something people could appreciate looking at, even today. Pimping afforded me a lifestyle that a regular job would not have been able to provide. I had family members and others who had good jobs, but who weren't able to travel like I did because they had to punch a time clock.

It was raining very hard as the ladies and I arrived in Atlanta. I remember a song playing on the radio called "Rainy Night in Georgia," by Brook

Benton. We turned into the hotel and I parked my red Cadillac, with gangster white wall tires in the hotel lot. I went inside and rented rooms for me and the ladies.

We took the opportunity to visit the underground. I put my ladies down on Peachtree Street and they made great money. I thought about where I wanted to go from there and decided on visiting Florida to see what it was like, but we ran into some trouble and never made it there.

We got up the next morning, dressed and prepared to check out at noon to head to Florida. There was a diner across the street from the hotel and we decided to stop and have something to eat before we got on the road. While we were in the diner there was a well-dressed, prosperous looking white man outside. One of my ladies went out to talk to him. They made a deal that they were going to go out.

Little did we know, there was a trap being set. As my lady talked to the man, he encouraged her to come inside and get another one of the girls because he had a friend in the car who also wanted to go out. My lady came back inside, got another lady and they all headed up to the hotel room. Some time went by and I decided they had been up there long enough. I was ready to get on the road and leave.

I went over to the hotel, went upstairs and knocked on the door. One of the men opened the door, pulled out his badge and said, "Come on in, we're the police." "Oh my God," I thought. I remembered my one lady waiting in the diner. The officer and I went downstairs to get her saying, "Everything is going well upstairs. They're having a good time. You might as well come on up too." She priced him and he brought her up. There I was, along with four of my ladies in the hotel room. The police thought all this was funny. They had one pimp and four prostitutes.

The officers took me and the ladies to the police station making jokes along the way. "Oh, this is a good day. We've got a pimp and four of his prostitutes!" We arrived at headquarters and bail was set at $65,000.00. "How is that so? I said." They told me, "Because you have out of town plates, they arrested you at the hotel with a room registered in your name, and these are your ladies." I said, "Pardon me sir? These are not my ladies." "Well, it's your license plate and your driver's license is registered to that room," he said. "So be it." I told him. "My license plate and driver's license may have connected me to the room in the hotel, but they don't connect me to the ladies you arrested." He said to me, "We'll see." The total bail was $65,000.00; $25,000 for me and $10,000 for each of the ladies.

They took us all to jail and locked us up. I wasn't nervous though, because I knew that all I had to do was make a phone call because I had my own bail bondsman. That was something that true pimps did in my time, they would make very sure they had a good lawyer and a good bail bondsman. I had them both.

When I made the phone call, I called my mother and said, "Mom, I'm down here in Georgia and I need $65,000 for bail." I gave her the number to call my bondsman, Sonny. I knew it wouldn't be a problem. All I needed to do was make the phone call and he was going to make sure that our bonds were secure. He knew Pimping Al was a business man and I needed to be out of jail in order to make money.

When they brought me to the jail cell, the inmates were looking at my hair and the way I was dressed. Word began to spread that there was a pimp from Ohio locked up there. Apparently they had something against pimps, as many people did and still do. They started making jokes and saying things like they were going to beat me up when the cells opened the next morning.

One man in particular started calling me all kinds of pimp names, saying pimps were girls and that pimps didn't fight men, only women. He said, "I'm going to kick your ass when they open the cell in the morning." The officer at the desk came back to my cell and said, "Don't worry about him. He's a hard working man whose here just about every weekend because he's always getting into fights." I said to the officer, "Sir. Could you do me a favor?" He said, "What is it?" "Could you please open his cell door, open mine, and go back to your desk and act like you don't see anything that's going on? I will kick his ass until I feel better." The officer said, "I would love to, but I can't do that."

The next morning when they were opening the cell gates this young man had done something during the night while I was asleep. I don't know what happened, but the officers were not going to open the gate for him. We were standing in line to go by his cell and he looked up and saw me coming by. He hauled off and spit at me right out of his cell and I immediately threw a punch directly at his face. I wound up hitting part of his face and part of the cell, injuring my hand which began to swell. The other inmates saw that I was no joke; that this man did not play. They began to give me what every man had to give me and that's respect, because I was man enough to demand respect.

40

When we went to court, an FBI agent came back and said to me, "Well, Mr. Howard we finally got you." I simply said, "Yes, you got me, but how long are you going to be able to keep me?" He said, "You're going to court and the ladies are going to court. We're going to take you before the Attorney General." I said, "Okay. You do what you have to do and I'm going to do what I have to do."

I had two lawyers working the case. The ladies went up first. Two were Black and two white. We went before the Judge and each lady stood up. He wanted to know if Mr. Howard had brought them there and if they were connected to the hotel room. They told the Judge that maybe they were connected to the hotel room, but Mr. Howard was not their pimp. The Court didn't have a case so they let me and all of the ladies go except for one, because they charged her with "pimping." It seemed they would go to any extreme just to lock somebody up. The remaining ladies and I got into the car and headed home.

Once we got back to Cleveland, I went to the bank, took out more money and called my lawyer. I asked him how much money I needed to get the lady out of jail. He said, "Right now it's not about money. They haven't set bail and are trying to get her to tell them that you are her pimp." They told her, "We don't want you, we want Pimping Al. If we get him we'll let you go. If you sign a statement, we'll release you, buy you dinner and fly you back to Cleveland." She looked at them and smiled saying, "You want Pimping Al? I want Pimping Al too! I don't have anything to say to you."

I already knew she was a strong woman. I believe she stayed in jail for another week. They realized they weren't going to be able to break her down, no matter what they offered her or what they were going to do. She was not going to put Pimping Al in any jail cell in Georgia.

They eventually had to release the woman. I went to the airport and purchased a pre-paid ticket. My lady got on that flight and flew out of Georgia into Cleveland Hopkins Airport. We went to the club that night to celebrate because she was so happy to be back. We partied all night.

Chapter 7

WEST COAST PIMPING

The problems in Georgia sent me back to the drawing board to draw up a plan and execute it. After being back in Cleveland for a while and checking on my children, I decided it was time to take my pimping from the east coast to the west coast. One of my ladies, Chris and I took a flight out to San Francisco. We settled into our hotel room and I told her to get some rest. I went out to look over the city and find the strips where girls were working.

I flagged down a taxi and got inside. The driver asked me, "Where would you like to go sir?" as he checked out the jewelry I was wearing. I told him I wanted to go to the Fillmore District. He said, "Oh no sir. You don't want to go up to the Fillmore District. That's where they have pimps, drugs and prostitutes." I kindly looked at the driver and said, "Sir, drop me off right there in the middle of that place because that's where I need to be." The driver drove me to the Fillmore District and I got out of the car. I walked around taking in the lights and the girls. It was an awesome and beautiful sight. There were pimps and their prostitutes all over the place and here I was standing right in the middle of it.

A Cadillac pulled up with a pimp inside. He looked at me standing there and let down the window and said to me, "I know you're a pimp. Where are you from?" I told him I was from Ohio. He said, "Oh, I've met a lot of pimps from Ohio man. You got some real players from Ohio. Come on get in." I got in the car with him and he drove me around the strip showing me where the girls were working and pointing out popular disco clubs. He finally looked over at me and said, "Come on man. There's much more work here on the west coast. Let's go across the bridge to Oakland." I was just sitting there sniffing my cocaine and feeling good, feeling real pimpish.

When we arrived in Oakland he took me to the strip and showed me the part of the strip where the white girls worked, and another area where Black girls were working. He took me to a diner where pimps would hang out and introduced me to pimps from all over the country. I fit right in and felt real good.

This man's name was Vlad and he was a hell of a pimp. He said to me, "I have ladies who work not just here in San Francisco or Oakland, but I have ladies working in Fresno, California as well, and they're doing real good down there. I can hook you up. I have a connection with a house in Fresno. I know your ladies are fine and you would do real good there as well, but there's not too much for a pimp to do in Fresno. You know how the police feel about us. They hate pimps. Pimps here usually hang out in clubs during the day or evening while their ladies are working."

I took a flight out of San Francisco and flew down to Fresno. I went to the place he told me about and it was awesome. My ladies were making so much money, but I didn't have anything to do but sit in a hotel room and sometimes grieve about my children back in Ohio. I had thought I would go to California for just a week and I would leave, but the money was coming in so well it was hard to do that.

Finally, needing something to do, I started going with some of the pimps to a lady's home where drugs were sold. I later learned the woman's name was Bernice, and that she was the actual drug dealer. Her man had been a drug king, and when he was murdered she took up the business and started selling the drugs herself. The pimps told me, "Al, man, this woman's got lots of money and she's making tons of money. We've been trying to get her, but she just hasn't chosen any of us. During the day we go there and we get high. Let's go up and we'll introduce you to her." They took me to the house and introduced me to the lady.

At first, I would just sit there and get high with the rest of the pimps, but I noticed that Bernice would treat me a little differently. Whenever I purchased from her she always tried to make sure that I had the best quality of whatever I bought. Eventually she and I had a chance to talk and she said to me, "A lot of these pimps come here and I know they're trying to get me. They want my money, but I don't particularly care for any of them, but there is something different I see about you. I like the way that you handle your business. I like the way you take care of your ladies. I wouldn't mind being with you." I said, "What?" Bernice said, "Yes. You appeal to me." I started to think things over.

I had planned to be there for a week, but I stayed a week longer. I had now been in California for two full weeks. I missed my children, so on Sundays I would call them back in Cleveland to talk. Sometimes after hanging up the phone I would cry because I missed them so much. Here I was on the west coast. The pimping was going great and my ladies were doing well. I was in the midst of a female who was making more money than maybe three or four pimps put together, because drug money came much faster than whore money.

I was trying to think things through, but at the same time I was doing more drugs without even realizing it. I eventually started doing heroin and one day just said to myself, "Oh my God." I had always thought that I would never do heroin. I would never shoot a needle in my arm, but here I was in California with these west coast pimps and I'm doing heroin.

After being in California for three weeks, Bernice took me into her bedroom, went into the closet and pulled out a vacuum cleaner. She opened the vacuum from the bottom and it was filled with stacks of one hundred dollar bills. She threw the money across her bed, looked at me and said, "All of that is yours and there is more. All you have to do is be my man. I know I can give you more money than those prostitutes can." I looked at her and had to tell her the truth. "Honey, I'm a pimp. I'm 100% pimp. Pimping is what I do. I use drugs but I'm not a drug dealer, and I don't want to be involved in that lifestyle."

For the first time I began to realize that it was time for me to leave and return to Cleveland. I stayed there for another week spending a total of one month in Fresno, California. I went out and bought a new car, a Buick Electra 225 with a leopard top. Back then people called that car a

"Duce and a Quarter." I got my ladies together and told them it was time to go.

Before we left we stopped by one last time to see Bernice. I told her that we were getting ready to leave and return to Cleveland. She was kind enough to make dinner for me and my ladies, and at one point she called them back into her bedroom. I didn't know what that was all about, but decided to ask the ladies about it when we got on the road. I asked them what they were talking about in the bedroom. They said Bernice told them to take good care of me because not only was I a good pimp, I was a good man as well. She also told them if we had any problems on the way back to Cleveland to call her, and that she would be there for us.

I wanted to do a little sightseeing before we left California. I had heard so much about Alcatraz, the prison where Al Capone was incarcerated, so we stopped by there. We also visited the Golden Gate Bridge where the ladies and I posed for pictures. As we made our way back east, we stopped by another placed I'd always wanted to visit, the Grand Canyon. The weather was so hot, even with the air conditioning on in the car, but we still had a wonderful time.

Once we returned to Cleveland my pimping friends wanted to know how things were on the west coast. The only thing I could tell them was that they had to go. It was something they had to see for themselves. My pimping lifestyle allowed me to visit many other places I wanted to see like St. Louis, Missouri and Denver, Colorado. I'm so blessed and thankful for my traveling experience. There are 52 states in the United States and I have traveled in most of them.

Chapter 8

REAL MEN HAVE REAL FEELINGS

Being a pimp for 30 plus years also brought a lot of sorrow along with it. Imagine having a stable of ladies one day, and then another you look up and the police have torn down doors and rounded them up, or arrested street walkers on the stroll. Situations like that weren't easy to deal with, but nevertheless pimping goes on and you had to stand up and continue to be a man. Can you imagine in your mind what it must really be like to pimp for 30 years or more? Just think about all the ladies who would come and go throughout a pimp's life during that time.

No matter how much of a "pimp" a man may be, a real man has real feelings. If a prostitute was around you long enough she often began to grow on you; you just naturally developed some feeling for her. Despite that, there may come a time when she gets tired of listening to what you have to say and turn her attention to another pimp walking on the strip. Most of the time pimps would simply say to another prostitute, "Don't you want to hear something new?" Maybe she could hear something from another pimp she had not heard from you. If she hears something she likes and is ready to move on, you must still be man enough that you can wish her well. You may have to walk around the corner and shed a few tears, but not let her see it. You have to keep on moving.

When pimps got hurt emotionally, we had to learn how to walk with our hurt and accept it. It wasn't always easy to have a stable of ladies with some of having been with you for 5, 10, or 15 years only to learn at some point that they're ready to leave. Not once has any lady who has ever worked for Pimping Al had to tell anyone that when she got ready to go she had to sneak off in the darkness running for a train, boat or a plane. When a lady got ready to leave Pimping Al all she had to do was leave. That was Al's way of pimping.

If a woman came to me like a lady I wanted her to leave me like a lady. There was no pimp who could ever say that Pimping Al showed up on his doorstep crying about how much he loved some lady who had decided to leave. When she left I understood and the only thing I expected from her new pimp was that he notify me that my lady was with him. Any time a lady would give another pimp my money I knew she was no longer with me. Whenever a lady left me I always said to the other pimp, "Be good to her. She paid me well. Maybe she'll pay you like she paid me." Nothing else needed to be said. That's the way Pimping Al conducted his business.

There are ladies who were with Pimping Al during the 1960s who have gone on with their lives and started families. Whenever we meet in passing those ladies still greet me with a smile, because Al was not the kind of pimp who would say bad things about a lady when she left him. I never said things like, "I hope she gets run over by a garbage truck." I'm not that kind of man.

Prostitutes didn't have holidays or days off. The only day off my lady had was the day she ran off. Sometimes I think they feel better just running off instead of telling you that they're leaving. Sometimes a lady will run off because she wants you to come after her but I never did that. I understood that prostitutes came to pay and not to stay.

Chapter 9

PIMPING AIN'T EASY

In the year 1970, Mary turned it loose and let go of the marriage. She divorced me and my pimping truly began. I was pimping in full force and not looking back!

My new lifestyle brought new things. Don't let anybody tell you that you can be a lamb in a lion's den and not be ate up by the lion. In my mind, being a pimp on Hough Avenue, there is no way you can deal with money, drugs, women and tricks without being a real lion. I know I was a lion because I had a lion's heart.

Being a pimp is not for everyone. My younger brother James always looked up to me as his big brother. At one point James decided he too wanted to become a pimp. I told him I didn't think it was a job that he could do, but he didn't listen.

He put this beautiful lady on the strip and decided to stop by the whore house one day. He opened the door and saw her having sex with another man. Jealousy took over and James was unable to accept what he was looking at. After that my brother took his lady friend home and that was the end of his pimping career.

There was also a time when my son Dwight told me he wanted to try pimping. I said, "Son, pimping ain't easy and I didn't think you're ready for it." Dwight persisted and even though I opposed it, he convinced me that this was what he wanted to do. He said, "Everybody says I look like you. I'm ready man." At the time, I was high on my cocaine and wanted to make my son happy. I looked over at my stable and picked out an attractive white girl for Dwight. I said, "Here, you can have her since you want to be a pimp." I talked to the woman and explained the situation. I told her that it was okay to go and make my son some money. I wanted her to help him out and she agreed.

That night the ladies and me, along with Dwight and his new lady got into the Rolls Royce and drove over to the strip on 8th Avenue in New York City. My ladies got out of the car and went to work. I felt hopeful that things would work out with Dwight and his new lady. She would make money for him and he could move on with his pimping career. As I got out of the car I heard him say to her, "Hold on. I want to talk to you about something." I thought he was going to talk to her about pimping or how to get his money so I walked away. About 10 or 15 minutes later I still don't see Dwight or his lady on the strip so I decided to walk back to where I had parked.

As I approached the car, I noticed that the windows were so foggy you couldn't see inside. I said to myself, "Now I know Dwight is not having sex with this lady right here on 8th Avenue and 44th Street!" Police hated pimps and if they caught my son in the car with a white woman having sex they would beat him to death. I called out to Dwight to get out of the car. The lady got out first. She was angry with me and Dwight. She took off and I never saw her again.

I said, "Dwight. What is the problem? You told me you wanted to be a pimp and I gave you a lady." He looked at me and said, "Well, I'm going to tell you the truth. I've never had sex with a white woman before so I just thought I'd try it." I said, "That's the end of your pimping career right there! You need to get on the bus and go back to Cleveland where your mother is, fill out some applications and get yourself a job." Today I'm happy to say that Dwight took my advice, went back to Cleveland and got himself a job. He's working two shifts and at least he's found out what works for him.

There are good and bad aspects of the pimping game and robbery was certainly a part of that lifestyle. I remember a night when my cousin Larry and I were riding down Hough Avenue. Larry likes to make jokes and he said something that at first I thought was a joke. He said, "Al Look! There's a lady running down the street with no clothes on!" I turned around but didn't see anyone.

As I rounded the corner of 84th & Hough my headlights hit a lady who was running down the side of the Astor Theater. It was one of my prostitutes, Patricia, running nude down the side of the building. When she saw my car she started screaming, "Al, Al, they're beating your ladies to death!" She jumped in the car and I asked her where they were. She told me they were behind the theater.

As I drove to get to the back of the theater, I saw another one of my ladies running with no clothes on, naked as she was when she came into the world. She was badly beaten and stopped briefly to lean against a light pole. As I stopped my car to get out and help her two cars blocked the street. At that point more of my ladies came running from behind the theater and they too had been stripped naked. As they started jumping into my car the guys blocking the street opened fire. I now had four ladies in my car and tried to take off. I couldn't go forward because the street was blocked so I tried to back up to get out of there. One of my ladies in the backseat yelled, "Al, don't let them kill you." My car was shot up with bullet holes and my windshield had been shattered.

I finally found a way out and sped down the street being followed by the men. I turned a corner a noticed some men standing outside on the porch of a house on Hough Avenue. They were Frank and Willie Taylor and my brother-in-law, Clyde Turney. They saw me tearing down the street and heard the gun fire. I knew I couldn't make it home because even if I did, I would have to get out of the car to make it inside to try and get a gun. My mind was racing about what to do. There was a Fifth District Police Station nearby on Chester Street. I decided to drive the car into the police station parking lot because I knew they wouldn't follow me there.

As I turned into the lot the car chasing me kept going. I waited there for a few minutes and then rushed the ladies to Mt. Sinai Hospital. Mind you, they're all in the car naked and had been beaten. I went inside the hospital and said to the nurse, "I've got four naked ladies out there in the car that have been beaten and robbed." The nurses were very kind. They ran out to the car with sheets which they used to cover the ladies up and took them inside the hospital.

I jumped back in the car and raced off trying to find somewhere I could get a gun. I needed to go back and try to find the people who had done this to my ladies. Everyone knew that Al did not play. You didn't mess with his girls, his money, or his children because if you did he would surely take you out of here.

As I made my way back I could see that the police had already caught the men. They were busted with guns, money and other things they had taken from the ladies. The next time Clyde and I had a conversation, he said to me, "Man, I thought that was it. I thought, Al is dead."

I once had a good friend named Steve Perkins. He was more than a friend to me, he was like a brother. I was pimping and he was selling drugs. I left town one day with my ladies and while I was gone someone robbed him for his drugs and drug money. Steve went to my father's home and asked him for my gun which I had left with my dad while I was out of town. My dad wouldn't give Steve my gun and Steve walked away disappointed. The last thing he said to my father was, "If Al was here, not only would he give me his gun, but he would go back with me."

A few days later, the young man who robbed Steve came back and found him in the same spot where he sold drugs. The man was carrying a gun and told Steve he was going to kill him. I was told that Steve said, "Man, forget about that mess. You've already robbed me and took the money." The man with the gun said, "No. I heard you were trying to borrow a gun to come back and take care of what happened early on." Steve started to run and the robber shot him in the leg. Steve fell down and rolled under a car. This young man came around the car as Steve rolled to the other side and shot him in the head taking his life. Steve died on the corner of 79th and Hough Avenue.

When I returned to Cleveland and heard the news, the first thing I did was go and pick up two of my guns. I set out to find the young man who had murdered my friend Steve, but couldn't find him. The police had already arrested him. Had I found him first I would have dealt with it as street justice. Thanks be to God that He allowed me to get around that part of the trouble.

Despite the violence, I somehow found a way to press on. I opened my own whore house and after-hour joint. After the bars would close my ladies would come off of the streets and come to my place of business. We would party until the sun came up. My friend Erving would take care of that part of the business for me. Erving would also go up on the whore stroll and look out for my ladies. He was the one who opened the door of the whore house so ladies could come in.

I recall one really bad incident happening at the house. One of my ladies brought two tricks in for a date. At least that's what she thought, but they had robbery on their minds.

On that tragic day, my friend Erving opened the door. As the gunmen entered, one pulled a gun and the other pulled a knife. They told Erving, "This is a stick up!" They demanded that my friend give up the money but he said, "No. I'm not going to give you Big Al's money." Arlene, one of my ladies said to the man who was holding the gun, "Come on baby. Let's go in the room. You don't even have to pay. We'll just go in there and have some fun." The man quickly spun around putting the gun in her face and said, "Shut up bitch! I don't want no pussy. I want the money!" He then turned to my friend Erving and told him, "I'm not here to play." Erving looked him in his eyes and again said, "I'm not going to give you Al's money." The man then shot my friend Erving with the bullet piercing him right under the heart.

Juanita, one of my other girls heard the shot from the other room and jumped out of the window. In the meantime, Erving was crawling on the floor holding the pocket with the money in it. The man with the knife also dropped to the floor and began cutting at Erving's hands and pocket. He eventually cut off the pocket, took the money and fled.

About 15 minutes later I drove up on the scene to find my ladies running and crying in the streets. They told me my friend had been shot and was taken to Mt. Sinai Hospital at the end of Hough Avenue.

I rushed to the hospital and when I walked into Erving's room the doctors were trying to get a tube down his throat. Erving looked around and saw me standing there. He said, "Al, I tried to hold on to your money." Oh my God. What a horrible feeling. I will never forget that day. The robbers had taken everything Erving had except 15 cents, one dime and one nickel. I took the dime and gave the nickel to my brother.

At that time, my brother was living with a young lady named Cynthia. We called her Kay. She and my brother also went up to Mt. Sinai to visit with Erving. The next day I got a phone call from the hospital saying I needed to come right away. Mary was throwing me clothes and I was trying to put them on as quickly as I could. I rushed into Erving's room at the hospital and kept saying to him, "Man, everything is going to be okay. Everything is going to be alright." Finally the nurse said to me, "He's gone." The only thing I could do was hold Erving's head in my arms saying to him, "I'm so sorry." To me he was more than a friend, he was more like family. He watched out for the after-hour joint and was shot in my whore house. The only thing left that I could do was pay his full funeral expense.

My life was full of violence, and several other friends who were also in the game were murdered as well. One of them, Benny Taylor, also known as Mr. T, used to work in Chris' Barber Shop until the game called him out. He started out as a drug dealer, and he too was a tall, nice looking man with long hair and the girls wanted to pay him. He went from being a barber to becoming a drug dealer and later became my friend.

After Benny's death, his son Benny, Jr. decided that since he looked like his dad he wanted to become a pimp too. Thank God Benny, Jr. met a lady named Deon who was not a prostitute, but a business minded woman. I'm so thankful that Benny, Jr. married Deon and decided against becoming a pimp. They are now both business minded people who are doing well. The last thing I was able to do for my friend Benny was to drive to

Alabama for his home-going service. I had to get permission from my parole officer because I had just recently been released from prison.

I will never forget Benny, Jr. He was too young to be my friend but he knew that I was his father's friend. He brought me a pair of shoes and he said to me, "Anything that you need until you get back on your feet just call me." I will never forget his kindness to me, and my prayer is that God will always bless him and the Taylor family. Chris Wright was our barber and so much more. He even went to the funeral parlor to do Benny's hair before they shipped his body to Alabama.

Years later my friend Freddie Tate was shot and killed by my wife's friend Veleria. Freddie was not a pimp. He was a hard-working, hard fighting man who fell in love with a beautiful woman that he could not let go of. Veleria was not just beautiful on the outside she was also beautiful on the inside.

Freddie and his family lived on the next street from us, which was 38th Street. He had a sister named Gloria who married a young man named Joe McDonald (Joe Mack), who I had great admiration for. These were the types of men I looked up to back in the day. Members of the Tate family were my friends then, now and always will be.

There is a lot of pain in the game. You need to be a strong man just to stand and be a pimp. You have to put your feelings in your shoes and walk on your feelings. The game, the heartaches and the pain are things you don't see on television when you watch movies about pimps. I remember seeing a young man who had been shot, running before he fell into a puddle of water on those mean streets in Cleveland, Ohio. I recall lifting that man's head from the water and watching him take his last breath.

These were people that I knew. They were men that I grew close to. They were closer than just friends and it was the love in my heart that drew me to them. They were real men who would stand up and face whatever came their way, but their lives were stolen.

I experienced heartaches and pain during my life that many people don't know about. They saw the beautiful cars that I drove, the clothes and expensive jewelry, but there was pain of which they never knew. My father said to me at a very early age, "Al, be a man, even if you have to be a dead man." I grew up with that in my mind and heart to be a man, always and forever.

The life of a pimp can also be a lonely one. Pimps don't have many true friends and are often disliked or hated by people. Although many people may surround him, there are few that he can really trust. Pimping is not a love game, it's a money game. People need to know that the stories they watch on television about pimps and prostitutes are fabricated in many ways. The real life of a true pimp holds a lot of bitterness. It's not as glamorous as it might appear to be.

True pimps are a dying breed. I'm not referring to men who put on monkey suits and stand around pimps pretending to be one knowing he is not. In the world we live in today, we have so many great pretenders, so many perpetrators and folks saying that they are someone they're not. There are men today calling themselves "pimps," but I'm here to tell you that many of them are lying. There are men who say they used to be a pimp and they're probably a used to be liar.

I know a real pimp when I see one. He doesn't have to open his mouth and say a word. If you need to say you're a pimp then I don't believe you are a pimp, because if you are one, somebody will know, simply by the way you carry yourself. People need to understand that true pimps are real gentlemen. True pimps know how to treat a lady, whether she's a prostitute, a housewife, a sister or a mother. The man in him will let him know who she is and he will automatically know how to treat her.

Chapter 10

SUPERFLY – PIMPING AND LOVING IT

In the 70's, my pimping career had taken off like never before. I remember that in 1973 I had my own business. I had Go Go Girls, Ho Ho Girls, Welfare Girls and Working Girls. I had a variety of ladies working for me and they only needed one thing - money. I didn't rob people. I didn't sell drugs. I was 100% pimp. I took care of my business and my business took care of me.

I made good money pimping and enjoyed sharing it with others. I was able to take care of my responsibilities and my family, not just immediate family, but my family as a whole. Pimping enabled me to help them along the way and I didn't have a problem doing so. I was a man who had a big heart and I didn't mind giving. As I received, I gave. Even today, I still have that same giving spirit. If you need something and I've got it, I'll share it with you.

One of the things that made "Pimping Al" unique from other pimps in Cleveland was that I believed a real pimp was a real pimp wherever he was. Another thing was the fact that I had a big heart. My heart was as big as all outdoors. This was not just a game that I learned how to play because I didn't have anything else to do. It was a livelihood for me. As I mentioned before, "pimping ain't easy," but life is not easy. Life is what you make it and so was pimping.

Like football, baseball or basketball, pimping for me was a game and the better you were at it, the better you were able to play. I had to learn how to play not just the ladies, because some pimps think that's all you need to know is how to play a lady, but I had to learn how to play for my life. Pimping was a life and death game. Any time you are involved in money, men and women you can rest assured that you'd better know what you're doing. One good thing about pimping is that no matter where I went across this country a real pimp knew a real pimp. A real man will also know a real man when he sees one.

A lot happened during the 70s. Mary Ann Turney and I re-married on September 18, 1973, and Albert Howard, Jr. was born on September 23, 1974. I was at the height of my pimping and on top of the game. I was making big money and truly having the time of my life.

I bought Mary and the children their own home on LaRose, right off Miles, and also purchased a home for my ladies in East Cleveland. During that time, the movie "Superfly," starring Ron O'Neal had just been released. Pimps were wearing long hair, long coats, sniffing cocaine and having their cars custom made. There was a shop in Cleveland called Roman Chariot on Superior Avenue. Roman was building custom made cars, mostly for pimps and drug dealers. I remember paying Jerry Roman over $53,000 to rebuild my custom 1974 candy apple red Cadillac.

I'm reminded of an event in 1974 that I'll never forget. My birthday was coming up on November 9th. I noticed that some of my ladies seemed to be doing things that were out of the ordinary. I was curious but didn't question them about it.

On the night of my birthday the ladies and I were hanging out, getting high and having a good time. Finally one of my friends said, "Come on man. We want to go to the Biscayne Lounge. Let's go by there." We walked into the lounge and I learned that my ladies had all gotten together and pulled off a wonderful surprise birthday party for me. I was amazed that they had taken the time to plan something so special.

The party was held in the Biscayne party room and hosted by Pat and Diane Olds. Some of the guests included my mother, Lula Mae Howard, as well as other family members. Also there were my friends, Slim Carter, Jerry Roman from Roman Chariot, Chris Wright from the House of Style and many others. The room was filled with people who had come to celebrate the occasion. There was plenty to drink and a delicious spread of food consisting of chicken, bar-b-que ribs and potato salad.

The highlight of the evening was the cutting of a 3-foot long cake, decorated with a picture of me standing next to my customized 1974 Fleetwood Cadillac.

Pimping Al was so well known at that time and the party was so big, that a reporter from the "Call & Post" newspaper was sent over to cover the special event. The Call & Post is a local Cleveland newspaper which is still in operation today. The reporter wrote a great story detailing all the excitement of that evening, and even took a nice photo of me at the party surrounded by some of my ladies.

There was no way the reporter could share the fact that the women in the picture were my prostitutes, so the caption under the photo read: "Al and his lovely hostesses." An event like that being reported in the paper was rare. It wasn't often that you saw a photo of a pimp and his prostitutes in the newspaper who weren't being arrested or hauled off to jail. What a night!

I knew that the story would appear in the newspaper the following week, and I didn't want my wife to learn about the celebration. Even though my wife knew the game I was in, I tried to give her and the children as much space as I possibly could concerning that part of my life. The day the story dropped, I went out into the neighborhood and purchased all the newspapers at the local stores and newsstands. I was trying to make sure that Mary didn't get a paper and see the story about the birthday party.

Despite my efforts to keep it from her, somehow my wife got the news about the party. She said my son Dwight had gone out to try and purchase a paper and there were none. Somehow the news got back to her anyway. She confronted me about the situation and said, "I heard about your big party celebration with all of your whores." I said, "What party?" She said, "There you go. There you go lying again. I know all about it, I just couldn't get the paper."

After the success of my party other pimps began having their birthday parties in different clubs as well, but they were nothing like the one given for Pimping Al.

Life was good and my name continued ringing all over town. Pimping, and all the ups and downs that go along with it, had truly started to consume me. I was doing drugs, prostituting women and doing a lot of fighting.

From the outside people would think things were going pretty well for me, but I was dealing with serious issues at home concerning my new son, Albert, Jr., who had been born "special."

Albert, Jr. had mental issues and I had a very hard time coming to terms with that. He was my son and I loved him, but after learning about his mental state I began to feel guilty. He was named after me, and I felt my son was born that way as a punishment to me because of the lifestyle I was living.

For two years my son couldn't talk. He just murmured. I was so afraid the world would take advantage of him; drug dealers, murderers, robbers, people who didn't show any love. I was afraid my son would be mistreated by these people. It's hard for me to admit this, but I had thoughts of killing him. I felt he'd be better off.

One night after doing drugs and getting high, I walked into the kitchen and saw my son sitting there. My mind told me to go upstairs, get a gun and take his life. I would leave a note for his mother requesting that she get a casket big enough to bury the two of us together with me holding him in my arms so I could always protect him.

My wife walked into the kitchen and saw me standing there staring at the baby. She snatched him out of the chair and said, "Why are you looking at my baby like that? What are you thinking? Don't even think about doing anything to my son because of the life you live and the people you hang out with." She said I needed to talk with a psychiatrist and I agreed. I wasn't in my right mind and I knew that. We made an appointment and took my son with us.

As the psychiatrist began talking, tears started to run down my face. I told him that I was only trying to protect my son. He asked me if I had any more sons and I told him yes. He said, "Do you think Dwight and Leonard could live in the same world that you live in with the same people you deal with? Do you think they could live in that world?" For the first time in my life I had to think about it. I told him "No." I didn't think they could. He said that if Leonard and Dwight couldn't do it, and with Albert Jr. having been born special, he would likely have problems with it as well.

I told the psychiatrist all about my fighting, shooting and drugging. I was crying like a baby. He turned to my wife and said, "You don't have to worry about him. He loves that boy so much."

My dad would say to me, "God has never let me down. That baby is going to talk. God is not going to let me die without hearing Little Albert talk." Eventually Albert, Jr. did begin to talk and my dad said, "Now I can close my eyes in death because God has answered my prayer."

That particular time in my life was bittersweet. My pimping career was at its highest, but I struggled with those issues about my son. God knew all about it and has found a place in this world Little Albert would be able to live in. It has freed my mind, and Albert Jr. has grown up to be a fine young man. He has never had trouble with drugs, alcohol nor has he ever been in jail. Today, Albert, Jr. works a job cutting lawns and has his own clientele of customers who call him "The Lawnmower Man."

After speaking with the psychiatrist it was much easier for me to move forward, but things were up and down at home. Mary started to hate everything about me that represented pimp, so she gave me an ultimatum at the end of the year that I would come home and be her husband and the father of our children. How could I come home when I had found out that I could earn $300,000 a year being a pimp? Mary could not understand that I was hooked on drugs and money. She was talking about me going to get a job, and I knew I was making more money than all of the men on our street who had jobs. I just couldn't do it. So, for the second time, Mary divorced me again, but God always has a ram in the bush.

I had been spending time with a young lady named Lynda. She was there through the second marriage and was hurt because she felt like I had married on her. She could have left like so many others did, but she stayed right there. She came away from the lifestyle I was living but we remained close.

There was a time when I had problems with the Cleveland Police Department. I had to kidnap Dwight, Leonard, Reta, and Lil Albert. I took them to Lynda's apartment and left them there with her. It cost her trouble trying to keep them for me. It's strange sometimes the way God allows things to happen.

Later in life I left Cleveland and Mary, but I never left my children. My ladies Lynda, Nicki and baby Alana left with me. My children would come from Cleveland to New Jersey to spend time with me. My children came to care for and respect Lynda so much that until this day, my son Leonard still calls Lynda his step-mom. She came from a godly family with sisters: Irish, Elane, Sandy, Beverly, Pattie, Tracey, Stephanie and Robin. I thank the Lord for those He allowed to be in my life. Lynda and Nicki's families were very good people.

Even as a pimp I remembered something my parents always taught me, to respect my elders. There were many ladies in my life and sometimes I look back and think about some of the mothers I met along the way, even in my wildest days; real mothers like Patricia Stephens, Mary Turney, Georgia Hodges, Sara Fish, Dorothy Lewis, Jean Bland and so many others. Even as a pimp I gained their respect.

The good Lord knows how much love and respect I have for the ladies' mothers. All of the daughters of these women were not prostitutes. They were in my life, but not in that particular part of my life. Patricia Stephens found out that her daughter Lynda was not in that part of my life, but was for the most part always in my life. I have learned how to thank God for those ladies that he placed in my life for such a time as this.

The Bible says in **Esther Chapt. 4:14** - *"For if thou altogether holdest thy peace at this* *time, then shall there enlargement and deliverance arise to the Jews from another place; but thou and thy father's house shall be destroyed and who knoweth whether thou art come to the kingdom for such a time as this?"*

Who knows why God allowed me to come to the kingdom for such a time as this, but God is an all knowing God and he knew that if he let me live I would declare his truth. My mother and all the mothers' names that I've mentioned have gone on home to be with the Lord, but God gave me enough time to get to know them and to love them.

Chapter 11

THE IMPORTANCE OF STYLE

Being in the game I learned a lot about personal style and grooming. These things are important, not just in the game, but in real life as well. There are benefits to being a well groomed person. What would you look like going on an interview for a job with run over sneakers, uncombed hair and smelling any kind of way? Who do you think would hire you in those conditions? Proper style and grooming should be a part of you.

Pimping was a competitive game so it paid to be well groomed, drive nice cars and have beautiful ladies. A good pimp had to strive for the best, because the best of him meant the best for his ladies. The better the ladies were, the more money we could earn. Pimping was a money game, not a love game.

When I first started out, I bought a lot of my clothing from a store called "Mr. Alberts," which was on St. Clair Street in Cleveland. Once I became more successful I started having my clothes tailor made and personalized for me.

It's nice to see other men, such as television and radio celebrity Steve Harvey, who once lived in Cleveland, Ohio, take pride in style and grooming. I appreciate the fact that we still have men in the world today who don't mind dressing up. I remember the times when I used to pull up on the strip or the whore stroll. There would be people standing outside the club when my ladies and I stepped out of my Rolls Royce. People would say things like, "There's Pimping Al and he's going to give us a dressing lesson." Even today in ministry, being stylish and well groomed is just a part of me. It is still a part of my life.

I've seen TV shows like "Jerry Springer" where young men who are poorly dressed with uncombed hair are claiming to be "pimps." That discourages me when I see that type of mess. My recollection of a pimp was a man who was very well groomed in every aspect of the word. He and his ladies were immaculate, as well as his cars and clothing. Seeing pimps and their ladies, just before the sun went down in the evening was truly something to see. Hollywood didn't have anything on the pimps of my day or the strips where the ladies worked.

Chapter 12

TROUBLE WITH THE LAW

At 34 years of age I had never been to prison. I'd been in jail cells all across the country, but never once had I been in a penitentiary. I started having problems with the law because my name was so big in Cleveland. All you could hear was "Pimping Al or "Prince Al." The police got tired of hearing that. They got tired of seeing Pimping Al with some of the most beautiful white women you could ever lay eyes on. Not only did they have beautiful faces, but they had gorgeous bodies and made lots of money.

How do you think the police felt about that? They see this Black man riding around all day and night in his custom made Cadillac, which was so beautiful it was featured on television and in auto shows. If he wasn't riding in that, he had his own pearl white limousine, with a chauffeur driving him around town. To top it all off, he had a big party given at a club with a picture of that red Cadillac on the cake. Of yes, you better believe Pimping Al took it to the limit!

In 1978, I moved to New Jersey for a couple of reasons. One was that I was having big problems with some of the men who worked the Vice Squad. In the Cleveland Police Department they were determined to take me down. They could not accept the fact that I had so many white women prostituting. There was a club that I used to hang out in, the Biscayne, just below 40th and Euclid Avenue. I used to work my prostitutes out of several nice clubs in town like the Capri, which was next door to the Cleveland arena, the Wine and Roses, the Malibu, the French Quarters and the Burlesque, just to name a few.

At the time I was making so much money that I would go to Mary's house and throw thousands of dollars on the bed saying to Dwight and Leonard, "Count this whore money." It made Dwight and Leonard happy to count whore money. Their mother would stand at the door with hatred in her eyes and say to me, "You are setting bad examples for your sons." I couldn't understand it then because I was too caught up in my pimping. I would take my sons to the club house, the bar house, and as they grew up I would take them to the drug house.

This one particular Vice Cop decided that he wanted to be a police officer and a pimp, so he brought this young white female to the Biscayne where I was very well known. He left word to tell all the pimps not to say anything to her. When I arrived on the scene she was on the stage dancing and smiling at me. I stood there smiling back and another pimp walked up and told me what the cop had said. I was not afraid of the police or anyone else because this was truly my livelihood.

I'm proud to say I was a pimp, no chaser. I didn't rob people and I didn't entice women to use drugs. My prostitutes were clean. The only thing they had on their minds was to get Pimping Al's money and they knew how I liked it. If you were to ask one of my prostitutes how Al liked his money, they would tell you Al liked it quick, fast, and in a hurry. He also liked lots of it.

This particular police officer fell in love with the way pimps looked, the way they shined in the darkness. I think he had dreams of one day becoming a pimp himself. A lot of men back in those days admired pimps so much that they would sometimes put on a monkey suit, stand next to a pimp and try to pretend like he was a pimp, talking that monkey shit and acting like a monkey. Just messed up the game so bad until people were walking around pretending that they were something that they could never be! I have a friend named Lonnie Johnson. He used the street name B.K.A. Slim Carter or the Big Mac. He would always say that when pimps are talking, monkey shouldn't be allowed in the conversation because he was a true believer that pimps were born and not made.

Back to the police officer who wanted to be a pimp. He left word that no one should say anything to the lady he had placed in the club, but little did he know, that very same night Pimping Al had taken his girl out of the club and they were on their way to Denver. When the police officer found out he was so upset that he put word on the street, "I'm going to kill that nigger cause' he took my girl."

The officer began to arrest all the ladies who worked on Euclid Avenue in his district that he knew were working for me. Finally he sent his friend, an undercover officer to bust my whore house which was next door to Fix Cleaners on Payne Avenue. It seemed like the timing was a bit too convenient, because Mary was very angry with me during that time. Law enforcement officials were never able to pin me down. They could pick me up, but they couldn't hold me.

There came a time when my wife and I were going through difficult times. Back when things were good between us we would have pillow talks about all kinds of things. I remember telling her about plans that I had made. I believe that after our falling out she decided to go down to the Justice Center and locate some of the officers that I had mentioned to her.

The police wanted me so badly that they would do just about anything to get me off the streets. It wasn't because I had hurt anybody or was selling drugs. It was simple, here was a Black man riding around 24-7 with all kinds of beautiful white women. They're watching this every day and night. They watched those white women running to the car to give their money to Pimping Al. It hurt their hearts. Not only did Al have beautiful women running up to his car giving him their money, Al also had a house set up with call girls. He was getting money off the strip, out of the house, and from his after-hour joint. Pimping Al was getting money all kind of ways and the police found it hard to handle.

Apparently, my children's mother and the police sat down at the Justice Center and she told them how she felt about me. She said she really didn't like me anymore and that it didn't matter to her whether they killed me or what they did to me. She told them she would feel much more comfortable with Pimping Al off the street because if they got me, that would give her leeway to her freedom. If they killed me she didn't have to worry about seeing me anymore. If I was locked up she

89

wouldn't have to worry about bumping into me. She asked, "What do you want me to do?"

They told her what information they had on me and asked about what she knew that could help them take me down. The police couldn't take me down by themselves. They couldn't even do it with the prostitutes' help. They went to my children's mother at a time when she wanted me down. They joined forces with her and she allowed them to break into her home. Although I had made the down payment on the house, I didn't want to put it in my name because of my occupation. I always believed that if anything happened to me, so be it. I wanted to go down by myself. I would dare not take my children or family down with me.

Mary had already left me some time before the day the police showed up. I wasn't alone that day and had a lady in the house with me. Since Mary allowed them to come in, they didn't have or need a search warrant. The police took me and the lady to jail. I'm just thankful now that they didn't murder me and say that I hung myself in the jail cell.

In the end, they gave me nine charges. The police charged me with three guns that they took out of the house, and many counts of prostitution. They also charged me with Assault and Battery on Mary.

Back in those days I was able to obtain a good lawyer whose name was Everett Chandler. He had been a police prosecutor so he knew that they were full of shit. He fought so hard for my freedom. The prostitute didn't go against me at the trial so they had to drop the charges. The three guns that they found in Mary's house, they had to drop those charges as well because the house was not in my name. I was sitting in the courtroom looking good and feeling real good.

There were also charges against me that were false. They found me guilty on an Escape charge. My attorney asked the Court how I could be found guilty of an Escape charge when I hadn't escaped from anywhere. The police officer was angry because I was doing my job. I didn't mean any disrespect to him. I was just doing what pimps do.

The jury also found me guilty on the Assault and Battery on Mary. They didn't have to find me guilty on that charge. I plead guilty to that because I knew that I was whipping a lot of people at that time. I was whipping boys, men and women. Anything or anyone that got in my way, they had a whipping coming. The jury had to dismiss all of the other charges because they could not find me guilty. Since I pled guilty to the Assault charge and was found guilty on the Escape charge the Judge sentenced me to six months on each. He ran them together so I wound up doing 1-5 years in prison.

I had so much money in those days that I was able to buy myself some time. The police officers involved in the trial were hurt in one way and happy in another. The hurt was that they were hoping they could get me 30 years or more and get rid of me forever, but God was sitting high and looking low. God knew that he had a purpose and a plan for my life, so the police were not able to get me 30 years to life. They were happy just to go back to the street and tell people that at least they got Pimping Al off the street for a little while and now they were the king of the pimps.

I came to New Jersey and bought myself a beautiful home on Hobert Avenue in the City of Plainfield. While I was living in New Jersey I connected with my friend Lonnie who was in the game, on top of the game and still pimping right there on Euclid Avenue. Lonnie was smart enough to know when it was time to get in the game and time to get out of the game. He and his companion Michelle are still together living the good life somewhere in Las Vegas.

I had about one year to be out on appeal bond so I set up my living establishment in New Jersey and went to New York to start my prostitute business. Soon my time ran out and I had to return to Ohio to serve my jail time. I found myself locked in a jail cell and a week later I was shipped out to a maximum security prison in Columbus, Ohio.

The walls were 40 ft tall. You couldn't see in or out, but God was still sitting high and looking low. One night I came to my prison cell and there was a letter from a young lady who had stayed down to the jail most of the day only to find out that I wasn't there. Her name was Deanie and she was another young lady who was a part of my life, but not a prostitute. She was the mother of one of my daughters. When she heard the news that I was back in a jail cell in Cleveland, Ohio she came to see about me. I think she felt like this was a time in my life when I wasn't pimping, but in trouble.

That gave her an opportunity to do something to help me, something she couldn't do in my pimping life. Deanie didn't want any part in that area of my life. I thank God that he placed it in her heart that every month of my prison term she would come from Cleveland by bus and bring my daughter. She would stay two days to bring me food and let me spend time with my child. I will forever be grateful not just her, but another friend, Belinda Humphrey, who also was not a prostitute. Even today, if I came to Cleveland and needed a place to stay Belinda's doors are always open.

The friendship will never end. Belinda's son Derick has recently gotten married and given his life to the Lord. Her daughter Tracey is living in Maryland and doing well with her life.

On December 8, 1980, I was released from prison, came back to New Jersey and started pimping in New York City. It didn't take long for me to get back into the game where I had left off, and I promised myself that I was going to be a bigger pimp in New York than I was in Cleveland.

Two years after being released from prison my pimping was back where I felt it should be and even better. I was meeting pimps and some of the prettiest prostitutes from all over the world. I was making plenty of money and having a ball. You know the devil will let you do well for a little while. But the Bible says in the Book of **St. John 10:10** – *"The thief cometh not, but for to steal, and to kill, and to destroy: I am come that they might have life, and that they might have it more abundantly."*

Chapter 13

NEW YORK CITY PIMPING

My son Dwight had a friend named Keith who called me to say he was coming to New York City and bringing a prostitute. My first question was, "Is she white?" His answer was, "No." I told him not to come because at that time all of my ladies were white or Hispanic. I didn't have time to babysit my son's friend or his prostitute.

One morning I had returned from New York and was sitting in my kitchen doing my drugs. Keith called me on the phone and said, "We're here at the airport in Newark, New Jersey." I hung up the phone because I had told him not to come. The day passed and later that evening Keith called again to say they were still at the airport. I could care less, but he told me that he had his two year-old son with him and on drugs or not, I always had love in my heart for children. Because he said a baby had been there all day I got up, went down to the airport and brought them back to my house.

What Keith did not tell me was that the woman had a drug problem, but none of that was my concern. That night when we got ready to go to New York I didn't want to expose the baby to that type of life, so I said to Keith and Belinda, "You can leave the baby here while you go over to New York and try to be a prostitute and a pimp."

Once we had the baby taken care of, we got in the car and headed for New York. Here I was with two wannabe's in my car. When we arrived there, Belinda got out of the car wearing some Peter Pan looking boots and a tam on her head. After a few hours she started to yell, "I can't make no money up by these white girls and I'm ready to go!" I looked her over and could see wonderful things in her. First of all, she had a clear, bright complexion and beautiful brown eyes. She had a small, but well built body and she knew how to talk to people.

I knew that with the right change of clothes and a real pimp in her life she could be a money getter and stand beside any white woman and get paid. Because of the love I have for my children, and since Keith was Dwight's friend, I would not make a move on Belinda.

After a while Belinda got a chance to look around and see some real pimps. She decided she could no longer be with a wannabe pimp and told Keith to get on the Greyhound Bus and go back to Cleveland. There was an opening and I stepped right into it, but because of the friendship connection Keith had with my son I couldn't let him go back to Cleveland broke.

I gave Keith $1,000 to get on the bus because it was truly time for him to get out of the way so a real pimp could help a real lady get some real money. Belinda hooked up with Al and took on the name "Lady Diana." In the next few years Lady Diana was paying Pimping Al like the house was on fire! She had taken off those Peter Pan boots and put on some high heels. She started stepping like she owned New York City.

From that point on, whenever I saw Diana in New York it was in passing. She was getting so much money that she only had time to give me the money and keep it moving. She would tell me, "I'll see you when I see you. I have other appointments lined up." Lady Diana had taken street walking prostitution to another level.

Some of Diana's clients included singers, public officials and athletes, not to mention those international folks with money. People tried to encourage her to come to Paris and start her own business. She was getting money in and out of the country.   More importantly, over time, our relationship turned into a friendship.

Lady Diana was a money getting figure for me and became a mother figure for our son. Back in those days some pimps didn't allow their ladies to have babies, because it was said that it would interfere with their money, or the children would be called Trick Babies. I never concerned myself then or now about what people think or say.

There is a television program called the "Maury Show." Most of the people who come there for DNA testing are not pimps and whores, yet it is so sad to see females come on the show with five different men and neither one of them is the baby's father. That little boy that I picked up from Newark Airport became my baby and his mother became my friend.

Lady Diana and I went on to raise our son and at the age of 17, six months before he graduated from high school, she decided that my time was up! She moved on with her life, but I'm proud to say that my son is now 30 years-old and still very much in my life.

I became a father figure to some of the children born to my prostitutes or other women I knew. Recently I was in an accident and my daughter Jaquetta had taken me to JFK Hospital in Edison, NJ. She was crying and so concerned. The doctors asked me who she was and I simply said,

"My daughter." The look on their faces told me that they were so amazed because Jaquetta is very much white. Her mother, Debbie, acquired the street name "Body" because she was truly a workout freak.

Chapter 14

THE DEATH OF A PIMP – A CHANGE IS GONNA COME

In the 1980's I was driving around in a Rolls Royce, a custom built Cadillac, and custom built Seville. I was wearing over $100,000 worth of jewelry, and had more than a $100,000 cocaine habit. I had over a quarter of a million dollar home which was almost paid for, and over a quarter of a million dollars in safe deposit boxes. I still had curls, drugs and the girls.

I thought that my pimp life would never end. We were told that we're pimps from the womb to the tomb, but I'm so glad that God didn't let me die believing that lie! Years back a songwriter by the name of Sam Cook wrote a song called "A Change is

Gonna Come." I didn't know it yet, but a big change in my life was about to come.

My mother had moved from Cleveland to New Jersey because she was failing in her health. When a change begins to take place, God will sometimes allow us to lose something or someone. Many people would have thought I had it all, but on February 27, 1995, God called my mother home. With all the things that I had, for the first time in my life I felt broke, alone and void.

There came a time when I began to realize that Pimping Al was dead. How did I know that? Because I am now a Bible reading God fearing man. The Bible says in **2 Corinthians 5:17** – *"Therefore if any man be in Christ, he is a new creature: old things are passed away; behold, all things are become new."*

The Bible lets us know in the Book of **Isaiah 6:1** - *"In the year that King Uzziah died I saw also the Lord setting upon a throne, high and lifted up, and his train filled the temple."* That Bible verse lets us know that in the year King Uzziah died, Isaiah saw the Lord. Sometimes many of us have a King Uzziah in our lives. My King Uzziah was my mother, because in the year that she died, for the first time in my life I had everything a poor Black man could ever think that he wanted.

My mother had always been an important part of my life, even when my wife divorced me or when prostitutes decided to leave, my mother was always there. When my children by my ex-wife would visit me and then get lonely for their mother and go back to Cleveland, my mother was right there.

It was during this time that I acknowledged, for the first time in my life, that I truly had a drug problem. I didn't know which way to go. I remembered growing up and my father being out of the home. My mother would read the Bible and cry out to God. Before she departed from this life she left this scripture with me and I will never forget it. You can find it in the Book of **Romans 8:31** - *"What shall we then say to these things? If God be for us who can be against us?"* I had to be in God's Plan.

After my mother died I fell into a deep depression. The devil started speaking to my mind saying, "Listen man. You've been snorting cocaine for long enough. Now it's time to put it in a pipe and smoke it." I needed to talk to somebody so I called my brother James who was, at one time, a crack addict. He had even gone to prison for burglary trying to support that habit. When he was released he made my mother a promise that he would never smoke crack again. I told James about my situation and he said to me, "You do whatever you want to do, but I promised our mother that I would never smoke the pipe again and I never will."

When I hung up that phone I began to think that if my younger brother could make my mother a promise and keep it, even in her passing, I was going to do something different because my mother never wanted me to be a pimp. Her desire was that I go to school and become a lawyer or doctor. She believed I had the ability to learn anything I set my mind to do.

There came a time when I found myself looking around at the pimps I used to ride with, talk to, sniff cocaine with, and go to the clubs with. A lot of them had fallen down and not because of the game or the prostitutes, but because they decided to smoke crack. Instead of being about their business they were somewhere hiding behind some wall or door smoking crack. Some of the prostitutes started smoking crack as well and sometimes shared it with their johns, getting them hooked. When crack hit the streets in the 80s everything turned around.

I thought I'd never have to worry about that problem because I always knew how to love myself. In spite of everything that was going on around me I always loved Al. Sometimes I'd see some of my old friends in the pimping game standing on the streets of New York City asking for change, looking to wash windows, or sleeping in the Port Authority Bus Terminal. I decided I loved myself too much to put myself in that situation. I thought about what it would do to my children if I became a crack addict. I just didn't want to go out like that.

I was a man before I became a pimp or a pastor, but I know now that the Jesus who died and hung on the cross for me has more power than all the men of the earth. Being a man is an important thing. The word of God says that God created man in his own image and in his likeness. What could be better than being created in the image of God?

The game has changed so much over the years. You rarely see street pimps, strips or "whore strolls" as they were called. It's not that pimping has died, because it's still very much alive, but prostitution has been taken to another level. The game is still being played but a lot of the rules have changed.

For example, you have different levels of drug dealers. You have the street level drug dealer who stands on the block and tries to make a transaction. Upper level dealers have clientele come to his home. The higher level drug dealers bring in drugs from other countries.

Prostitutes come in different levels as well. You may not see them walking the strip anymore, but they're still working. Some work through "Escort" services or internet websites which are run from indoors. There are high level prostitutes who charge as much as $500.00 per hour. Some people may open up a house and put in beds to be used by prostitutes. You also have your madams and brothels. Yes, prostitution is alive and well and I don't think it will ever die.

There were many others in the game with me back then who are not here today, but God allowed me to live long enough to tell the story. This book is not about a pimp, drug dealer, prostitute or con man. This book is about the transformation power of God. Many years ago I was approached to write a book, but I had no interest. Now God has allowed me to live long enough not to just write a book about pimps and whores, but a book about the power of God, and how that God can take nothing and make something out of it.

I prostituted women, but I refuse to prostitute the word of God. The Book of **Job 26:7** reads - *"He stretcheth out the north over the empty place and hangeth the earth upon nothing."* That chapter and verse ought to let the world know that if God has the power to hang the earth upon nothing, then He has the power to take a man that is made from the dust of the ground and turn him into something.

I've heard many Bible stories, but I believe it's time to tell the Bible truth. Let me begin by saying that I found in the word of God that Jesus Christ, God's own son is the truth. In **St. John 14:6,** Jesus himself said *"I am the way, the truth,* *and the life: no man cometh unto the father, but by me."*

I had always told people that it was my way, the highway, or no way, but Jesus came into my life and let me know that He was the way. To begin the transformation power of God we must first learn how to accept the fact that we are all sinners and need a Savior. No matter how good we might think we are the Bible says in the book of **Isaiah 64:6** - *"But we are all as an unclean thing, and all our righteousness are as filthy rags; and we all do fade as a leaf; and our iniquities, like the wind, have taken us away."*

Once you try God you will find that he's sweeter than honey in a honeycomb The Bible let us know in **St. John 10:10** – *"The thief cometh for but to rob, steal, kill and to destroy."* I'm so glad that God has allowed me to understand his word. The thief is the devil, and I know that the scriptures are true. Look around in today's world. The devil is stealing people's lives, their joy, and he's destroying families.

I'm glad to have the word of God in my heart. When you get the word of God you get the power of God, and you're able to cast the enemy back into the pits of hell from which he came. I don't have to let him steal anymore. He stole too much from Al. He stole my family. He stole my mind. Any time that you are on drugs, your mind has been stolen. He stole my freedom and placed me in a prison.

Pimping Al is indeed dead and has now become a new creature in Christ, whose name has been changed to Pastor Albert Howard, Sr. God has a thing about changing people. The Bible let us know that God changed Saul's name to Paul and there were others in the Bible whose name God changed. The transformation power of God had to take place for the change to come.

I thank God for a saved and holy ghost filled woman named Mildred Jones, a member of the Pentecostal Family Prayer Center. I call her my philistine friend. Mildred would hear my testimony in church about how I used to live my yesterday life and she would say, "Pastor Howard, there is no way that I would have ever dreamed you were like that. Seeing and knowing the godly man that you are today only God could have made that change." I thank God for my friend and member of my friend's church, Dr. Pauline Elizabeth Ballard.

My mother had a sister named Airlean Pierce. Her husband was the Pastor of New Light Baptist Church on Hazelwood Place in the City of Piscataway. He was a man that God had blessed with much wisdom. I began spending more time with my aunt because she reminded me of my mother. Between my uncle and aunt praying for me and encouraging me to come to church, I started to find peace in the church and kept coming back.

There were times when I would walk into the church with two white women on one side and two Black women on the other. I didn't pretend like I had changed. I remember reading a scripture in the Bible, **Revelations 22:17,** which read: *"And whosoever will let him take the water of life freely."* I took that to mean that I could come as I was, and that is so true. We can come as we are, but we can't stay that way.

The Bible also let us know in the Book of **Romans 3:23** *"For all have sinned and come short of the Glory of God."* Jesus did not come to earth looking for saved folks. The gospel of **Luke 19:10** let us know that, *"For the son of man is come to seek and to save that which was lost."* Sometimes I hear folks say, "Pastor Howard, I'm so glad that I found Jesus," but I'm here to tell the world that Jesus was never lost we were.

I know today that the old things have passed away and behold all things have become new because I don't think like I used to think. God gave me a new mind so I don't walk that same walk, neither do I talk the same talk. David said in **Psalm 119:11** – *"Thy word have I hid in mine heart, that I might not sin against thee."*

I didn't know it then, but God was calling me out of darkness into His marvelous light by way of the New Light Baptist Church. It was a small church with a big heart. On March 8, 1998, Pastor Rev. Shelly Pierce allowed me to have what they called my trial sermon. God has allowed me to know that it was my first sermon. In time, Pastor Pierce presented me with an evangelist license to go out into the world. In **Mark 16:15**, the scripture says *"Go ye into all the world and preach the gospel to every creature."*

Back then, I was unable to grow in God's grace because I was too busy fighting with my family. New Light Baptist had lots of family members. Pastor Pierce's two granddaughters, Mary & Patricia and their brother Mark could not find it in their hearts, even though I was older, to respect me truly. I think it was because they didn't see any change in me. They could only see the house that I was still living in, and the ladies I brought to church. They couldn't see what was in our hearts. They did not have enough of the love of God in their hearts to help us get right with God.

My cousin, Evangelist Mae Ruby Shepard was their mother. She lived down the street on Hobert Avenue, but belonged to another church, Temple of God and Christ where Amos Jackson was the founder and Pastor. She was in the middle of all this. Her father was the Pastor of the church, but her three children and her cousin just could not come together. Today we still have a lot of folks in the church who don't have enough love of God in their hearts to try and help someone. But the Bible says in **St. Matthew 7:1** – *"Judge not that ye be not judged."*

The spirit of God led me to a church in the City of Newark, New Highway of Holiness, where the Pastor and Bishop had love in their hearts. Pastor Joannie Baskerville welcomed me and my family with open arms and lots of love. Her husband Bishop Baskerville taught us the word of God, but for myself I can truly say that he taught me how to be humble. I stayed under their ministry for about five years.

On June 24, 2000, Bishop Baskerville gave me my ordination papers and soon thereafter God called them to LaGrange, GA, where Pastor Joannie Baskerville is the Pastor of the Rising Grove Baptist Church and Bishop Baskerville is the teacher of God's word. The people there are blessed to have them. In the year that I was ordained, God touched Pastor Willie D. Walls of Mt. Zion Church to give me the opportunity to come by and preach a 5-night revival. I've been there every year since that first invitation.

Chapter 15

If You Want to Get Hurt, Go to Church

My transition from pimping to pastoring was not a smooth one. I thought church folks would open their arms and welcome me with love but that just didn't happen. Early on many of them said such negative things about me. Back then I didn't have the strength or power I have today, and I felt overpowered by what seemed like demonic spirits. Before I became stronger I was so hurt, so tired. I was just all messed up.

People would say things like, "Oh, look at him in the pulpit. There's a pimp in the pulpit!" Some would tell people not to give me their money and that I was a fake pastor. My feelings were hurt and it was painful to hear those comments, but by the grace of God and people who loved God enough to pray me through, now I know those people were wrong when they said there's a pimp in the pulpit. In reality there's an ex-pimp in the pulpit because that's what I am, an "ex" pimp. I'm also an ex-inmate, ex-drug addict, as well as an ex-husband. When you come to Christ and give your heart to God then God just removes all of those "exes" and you become a new creature. Former things have passed away, behold all things have become new.

This God that my mother had told me about was a God of love, so I thought that once I made my way to God's house it would be different than it was in the drug house. In reality, I found out that people who are in the whore houses and drug houses sometimes show more love than people in the church house. For example, you can go down on skid row and find a wino and his buddies sitting on the ground with one bottle of wine. They will share that bottle of wine with each other until it's empty. Going into the church house you find people who profess to love God and tell you they're saved, sanctified, holy ghost filled, fire baptized and speaking in tongue as God gives them utterance.

If you can look around in the church and find 40 people who will share their last with you, I'll give you an amen praise. If you can walk into a church and find 10 people who don't hesitate to reach out to you with love then I'll give you another hand praise. Sometimes you'll find church folks who won't even share their phone numbers with one another, but they say they love each other. Oh, I tell you, if you want to get hurt, go to church.

At one point I was so hurt I was ready to give it up. I was ready to walk out of that church because I saw that people in the drug house, whore house, or prison house were more real than some people in the church. It's still going on today, but what's important is that we get stronger in the lord because with God's help we are able to stand, but if we try to do it alone we'll never make it. The Bible tells us in **Matthew, 19:26** – *"With men this is impossible; but with God all things are possible."*

Some church folks are truly good at hurting the feelings of other people. But the Bible lets us know in **1 John 4:8** – *"He that loveth not knoweth not God for God is love."* I thank God for his love because when folks said that I wouldn't amount to anything God's love said differently.

We have so many people in the ministry today who don't have the spirit of God on the inside. Ministry has become big business, but it shouldn't be just about business. Today the focus seems to be on the "mega church," "megafest," and "mega mess." Many people are just looking for the "mega dollar," but it shouldn't be that way. I believe that ministry should be about lost souls.

You have to stay prayed up because it's not the people in church who are going to help you get your life right. When you get in the word of God and let the word of God get in you then you become the church, and that place is just a building where you go to worship God.

Throughout my pimping days, although I didn't realize it at the time, I now know for sure that what I went through was an experience God allowed me to have. It was a life experience. I believe God allowed me to have that particular life experience of meeting all kinds of people, traveling to different places and being exposed to so many things so that it could be of use to me today. Those experiences have proven to be assets in my ministry. I'm able to interact with all kinds of individuals because dealing with people, places and things have played such a large part in my life. While I was a pimp, I was exposed to millionaires, entertainers, professional athletes and so many others.

Today, there are people coming into the church from all walks of life. I believe God gave me the name for my church, "The New Beginning Outreach Ministries for All People," because I've connected with all types of people throughout my former lifestyle. For me, the phrase "new beginning" is meant for people who are tired of being tired. That's what it took for me. There came a time when I became tired of being "Pimping Al," and started to look for something different, something new, a new beginning. No matter who you are or where you come from, God is able to give you a new beginning too.

When God calls you he certainly puts his love in your heart, so I'm able to love God's people and it's not because of what they can do for me or what they can get from me, but what I can give to them. I'm grateful that I'm able to give back. What can you give to anyone that's more important than the word of God? As a pimp I gave ladies diamond rings, Cadillac cars, homes and fur coats, but there is nothing I could ever give to a woman, man, boy or girl that is more important than the word of God. In the word of God there is life and I'm so glad that I'm able to give life to the people.

God can take nothing and make something out of it. God can stop a pimp from pimping and I know he can because he stopped me from pimping. I'm a witness. God can stop a drug dealer from dealing drugs. He can also stop a drug addict from being a drug addict. I know this for myself. All you have to do is come to a place where you're tired of being tired and realize that you need a change in your life. No matter how much money you have or what kind of status you hold we all need Christ in our lives. No Christ, no life. I'm thankful now that I was once lost, but now I'm found. I was blind, but now I see.

No matter who you are, where you come from, or how low you might be, just know that the

God who saved me is still sitting on the throne. He still has an all seeing eye and is a God of love. He loves everybody, but everybody needs to learn how to love God. I'm so thankful today that I did not die out there in that jungle, because that's what it is.

Today I'm so glad that I didn't give up on the church. I had people in my life after I came over from the other side who knew God and loved him, and with the love of God, you will help the people. The Bible says that if any man be in Christ he is a new creature. I know today that I am a new creature and I thank God for that. I thank Him for his love and the fact that he loved me so much that even when I was a mess, God had the power to come down in the midst of my mess and clean it up.

I've always been fortunate enough to be where I needed to be, and even today I'm where I need to be in the lord. When you take a look around, we all need to know that it's time to get right with God and the time to do it is now, because tomorrow is not promised to any of us.

Chapter 16

THE TRANSFORMATION

When God turned me around I was able to help somebody else. The prostitutes used to follow me to the drug house and the whore house, but when I turned my life around they began following me to the church house. I'm glad about that, as well as the fact that I was able to bow out of the pimping game gracefully. I didn't leave because I was old, raggedy and drugged out. I left the game because I was tired of being tired. My mind was all the way gone.

Today I can look back and thank God that He gave me a new way of walking and talking. That old pimp mind and drug mind I had are gone. God had a new mind in store for me according to **Romans 12:2** which reads - *"And be not conformed to this* *world: but be ye transformed by the renewing of your mind, that ye may prove what is that good, and acceptable, and perfect will of God."*

God's love saved me. Jesus said in **2 Corinthians 12:9** – *"My grace is sufficient for thee."* Surely I can be a witness today that it was God's grace that saved me for it was nothing good that I had done. His grace was made perfect in weakness. Most gladly therefore I would rather glory in my infirmity that the power of Christ may rest upon me. By the renewing of my mind and the transformation power of God I am no longer conformed to this world, but transformed by the power of God.

I wanted something new and different in my life, and I couldn't find it anywhere or in anyone except Jesus. That's my advice to anyone who may read a page from this book, that you might understand that I'm not trying to write a book because I deserve glory or honor, because I don't. God deserves all the honor because the glory is already his. The word of God is a powerful word. The word of God can change things. It can make things right in our lives.

It's unusual to hear about a pimp bowing out gracefully when he is at the height of his pimping. When I left the game for the second time, my pimping was going strong. I remember when prostitute, Lady Diana, tried to get me to change my mind about leaving the pimping game. She said to me, "Al, why don't you come back. Those church folks aren't going to give you the kind of money you get in the game." I had to tell her the truth. I said, "I can't come back hon, I'm gone. I've found something better." Diana said, "Well, I guess that's the way it is, but I just want you to know that I'm going to stay in the game just in case you need me one day."

Lady Diana stayed in the game for a while and thank God, sometime thereafter, she left the lifestyle too. She was a faithful prostitute for Pimping Al for over 17 years. Diana is now back in Cleveland, doing her own thing, working a job and serving the lord.

I was committed to getting myself together. Sometimes change is so hard for many people. We get used to doing the same thing for so long. The same person doing the same thing, going to the same places will never change. I thank God for the change that came in my life. The book of **St. John 5:30** reads – *"I of my own self can do nothing."* Today I would just like to set the record straight. Al of his own self found out one day that he could do nothing of his own self. Had it not been for God I would have been dead sleeping in a watery grave, but because of God's grace and mercy He looked down from his holy hill and had mercy on my dying soul.

My sister Laura came to New Jersey to visit a friend. While she was here she met and married Horace Burris. Mr. Burris became my brother-in-law and Laura became an evangelist. During this time I was a drug addict and Mr. Burris was an alcoholic. We didn't get along very well in those days but think about it, drug addicts and alcoholics just don't mix. I'm thankful for a merciful God, because Mr. Burris is no longer an alcoholic and I'm no longer a drug addict. Today I can truly say that I love my brother-in-law because we put down the drugs and alcohol. Mr. Burris has since given his life to the lord and is a faithful member of a local church here in the City of Plainfield.

I have learned firsthand, that what we are today does not determine who we will be tomorrow. Because of the love I received from my parents, even in all my madness, there wasn't anything or anyone that could break that strong bond of love I had in my heart for my children and family. When I look back over my life I can truly understand why my children's mother has moved on. How can you love anyone that is unfaithful? Can a pimp be faithful? I don't think so.

Mary Ann has met and married a fine man named Eli. She always wanted a man with a job and I do believe she got that part of her wish, because her new husband has been punching a clock for over 30 years. I never married again, but for the most part I believe that I have always been blessed. I found out that there is nothing better than to be blessed by God. When I think about where God has brought me from I am so grateful and thankful because God didn't have to do it but he did it anyway.

On several occasions, years ago, my friend Chris who owned the barber shop would tell me I was going to be a preacher. I didn't understand it at the time, and asked myself how he could say such a thing. I was pimping and had just started doing drugs. How could he say that I was going to be a preacher? As the years have gone by, it's very clear to me now that God has his own plans for our lives, whether we know it or not.

I am happy to say that at this point in my life, I have preached the gospel in so many different places. I'm so thankful that God allowed me to go back to Alabama where I was born. My uncle, Deacon T.C. Vincent showed me the place where my mother grew up. He was my mother's brother, and my cousin Cecil Vincent was the Pastor of a church. There were so many family members who were there, and I met a young lady named Lorene

Jordan. We exchanged numbers and became friends. She is such an encouraging person. At times when I felt like giving up she would call me and pray with me on the phone, or we would just make jokes about her old name, "Tootsie." We are still friends even until this day.

Mary Turney, my ex-wife's mother, saw the change that God had made in my life and wanted me to come back home and preach the gospel. She and her husband Dennis arranged a preaching engagement for me back in Cleveland. This was the first time since God had allowed me to be in ministry that I was able to go back to those mean streets in Cleveland, Ohio – not as "Pimping Al," but a new creature. I was born again, saved by the blood of Jesus.

Believe it or not, I was so afraid thinking nobody was going to show up because they were going to remember my past. The church was right down the street from where I used to work my ladies and where many violent fights took place. To my surprise the church was full inside and out. People came to see how God really changed this man, and God has truly blessed Pastor Howard. My motto is, "Get in the word and let the word get in you." The word can do anything but fail. We fail God, but He never fails us.

Pastor and Bishop Baskerville also invited me to LaGange, GA to preach the gospel. God has opened so many doors since I've become the founder and Pastor of New Beginning, located on South 10th Street in Newark, New Jersey. God has allowed me to be the Pastor there for the past 6 years. God will make a way out of no way.

I was not looking to become a Pastor, but I was preaching out of a church called Last Day, led by a great man of God, Pastor Bobby Wright and lovely First Lady Maxine Wright. I would do a lot of preaching at their church. Pastor Joannie Baskerville introduced me to them and Sister Barbra Sample would take me by there to preach 5-night revivals.

I once met a young lady named Denise Williams at the Last Day Church sitting next to Sister Wright. She was so angry looking and I later found out why. She had a drug problem, but Pastor Bobby Wright and his First Lady knew how to help a drug addict get off drugs through the word of God.

God called Pastor Bobby Wright home, and his wife asked their daughter Melody to call and ask me if I would come over to help. I said yes because they had always been so kind to me. When Last Day closed, Sister Maxine Wright and Sister Edgie Johnson were moved by God to help me to start God's church. This is how I officially became the Pastor of a church and God gave me the perfect name for it, the "New Beginning Outreach Ministry for All People."

After Pastor Bobby Wright went home to be with the Lord, Sister Wright and Sister Williams joined the New Beginning ministry. Sister Wright stayed there until God called her home. Sister Johnson doesn't attend very much anymore because of her traveling situation. God has now taken the drug problem away from Sister Williams and has called her to become the Deaconess in this ministry. A short time thereafter God called her to become an Evangelist and surely now she is working for the Lord, touching the souls of people like myself and so many others, who need to know that Jesus lives and because Jesus gave up the ghost, we were able to give up dope.

I am just so grateful for the faithful people that God has sent into the ministry who have stood by me: Sister Maxine Wright who was there from the opening door, Sister Edgie Johnson, Bishop Dillard, Bishop and Mother Marsh, and so many others.

Before I became a Pastor there was a family I knew in Plainfield, the Spanns, who lived on East Front Street. I would stop by their home and we would read the Bible and pray together. One day God gave Mary Spann a vision and she came to my home and asked me if I would teach her more about the Bible. She came with her daughter Michelle and son Williamson, and the New Beginning Bible School was birthed on March 26, 2006. I have been teaching the Bible school for eight years now, and I thank God that through teaching His word I've been able to give back some of what I have taken. I remember my mother saying, "Son, when you help somebody your living won't be in vain."

There is a Pastor by the name of Elder Letroy Pettigrew. He and his lovely wife, Evangelist Ruth Pettigrew started a mission on Lenagrave Avenue in Cleveland, Ohio called Miracle of Faith. They gave me the opportunity to come back home and preach a 5-night Revival. I cannot express in words how good I felt when I stepped up to the pulpit and looked out at the congregation. I counted 38 people from my own family who were there on the first night. My cousin Odessa Goodgame who I grew up with was there. She too has given her life to the Lord. It was good to see her daughter, Prophetess Lawana Jones, and her husband Elder Pete Jones in the building. I wish I could name all of the relatives there that night, but even though I don't mention all their names I love every one of them who showed up to support me. I even thank God for the Pastor of Fair Temple and all his members who came out to support the revival.

I was just on the phone a few days ago talking to another ex-pimp, a young man out of Memphis, TN named Cleveland Brown who has also given his life to the Lord. When Cleveland and I talk we don't talk about pimping, we talk about our new life in

Christ. Pastor Pierce has a son named William. He and I have always been very close. We grew up together outside of the church, but William has picked up his Bible and made a u-turn in his life as well.

In my new life God is bringing in people like myself who need a new beginning, people like con artist, Bobby Reid, who has embraced the Islam faith, but comes by the church to learn more about Jesus. Sometimes he will talk about 8th Avenue in Manhattan and bring up names like Buck and a few others that are still around. Mr. Reid realized that it was God who has kept us. God is sending in people from all walks of life and I feel so humble that God allowed me to live long enough to declare his truth. Even though I did not set good examples for my children, the one thing I can be very proud of is the fact that I have always been able to have a relationship with them and show them a heart full of love.

The only child that I don't have a relationship with is not by my choice, but hers, but I still love her as much as the others. God has filled my heart with His love and I cannot help but to miss spending time with my grandchildren and my great grandchildren. God did allow my granddaughter, Ashley Henry, to come to New Jersey after God had changed my life. Now with God's help I have learned how to set good examples for my children and my grandchildren. I was able to encourage Ashley to go back to school and complete her education. At the time she was married to a young man named DeVal, and I'm glad to say that the first day my church opened they were there.

Ashley is the daughter of my son, Leonard Howard, who has spent over the last 22 years of his life in a prison cell. People had asked me to write a book before now, but I never gave serious thought to any of that. But now that my son has become a writer and has given his life to the Lord, he has inspired me to write this book. Leonard and I are very close. I visit him every year without fail. When he told me that he had given his life to the Lord, words will never be able to express the joy that I felt. My son once said that after spending 22 years of his life in a prison cell, and going to church and learning about this Savior whose name is Jesus, he came to understand that gangsters don't live long but God lives forever.

I'm proud that God has encouraged my church members, Praise Minister Tiray Summers, sister Niya and baby Tianiya to be so faithful in this ministry. I believe it is safe to say that God has so many great things for all of us but there is a requirement. We must get right with God and we must do it now because tomorrow may be too late. If we die and our soul is lost it's nobody's fault but our own.

There is a young lady that I met out of Akron, Ohio whose name is Renee Singleton. When I met her she was truly on fire for the Lord. She has relocated to Atlanta, GA and is still on fire for the Lord. She told me a few years ago that I should write a book after she learned my testimony. I'm so grateful now that her words have become a reality. I thank God that He has allowed me to not just become a preacher of His word, but a teacher as well.

The word says in the Book of **Proverbs 18:16** – *"A man's gift maketh room for him and bringeth him before great men."*

Truly God's gift has made room and brought me before great men and women of the gospel. I would like to take this opportunity to thank and acknowledge some of them. Sadly, some have gone home to be with the Lord:

Pastor Dr. Pauline E. Ballard
Pastor Mary Barber
Pastor Willie Barber
Bishop James Baskerville
Pastor Joannie Baskerville
Evangelist Josephine Baskerville
Deacon Charles Baskerville
Dr. Julia Bogan
Evangelist Laura Burris
Pastor Bernadine Byrd
Pastor Marie Green Carr

Helen Lawton Douglas
Pastor James Dunlap
Apostle Kenneth Flowers
Evangelist Ida Flowers
Evangelist Henrietta Goodson
Rev. William Hill
Pastor Amos Jackson
Pastor Tom Jackson
Pastor Ruth Johnson
Bishop J.P. Lucas, Jr.
Dr. Margaret Lucas
Pastor Dr. R.L. Lumzy
Evangelist Dolores Lumzy
Bishop Leslie March
Overseer Pastor McClain
Deacon Walter McClain
Pastor Willie McMillian
Rev. Dr. Willie Muse
Elder Letroy Pettigrew
Evangelist Ruth Pettigrew
Bishop William Pickett
Deacon Nathaniel Pickett
Pastor Rev. Shelly Pierce
Bishop Purnell
Pastor L.C. Redding
Apostle Janet Smart
Deacon Sutton
Evangelist Alma Swoope
Pastor Mirranda Townsend

Pastor Willie D. Walls
Pastor Beverly Williams
Evangelist Beverly Williams
Evangelist Denise Williams
Evangelist Margaret Winn
... many more

There are so many other names of great women and men of God that I would like to mention, but God knows who they are and I am so grateful that God has given Pastor Albert Howard, Sr. a gift. The word of God said in the Book of **James 1:17** – *"Every good gift and every perfect gift is from the father of lights with whom is no variableness neither shadow of turning."*

Before I gave my life to God I had trouble with my wife, the police, and just about everybody else, but I found out in the word of God in **John 16:33** – *"These things I have spoken unto you that in me ye might have peace. In the world ye shall have tribulation: but be of good cheer; I have overcome the world."*

So long as I was in the world, I had trouble with just about everybody in it, but when I turned my life over to the Lord I got out of the world and into the word. Every since that time I have been done with the trouble of the world. Jesus said in the Book of **Philippians 4:7** – *"And the peace of God which passeth all understanding shall keep your hearts and minds through Jesus Christ."*

I don't have any more problems with my ex-wife or the police department. As a matter of fact, most of the officers here in Plainfield respect me as Pastor Howard, and I feel proud to say that I have met and become friends with Police Chief Michael Lattimore, as well as Mayor Sharon Robinson Briggs, Councilwoman Ethel Conry of Washington, NJ, and so many others.

I am a witness that since I came out of the world I came out of tribulation. I found out that Jesus meant just what He said. When He said that He would give me the peace of God which would pass all understanding, I'm here to be a witness that now I feel the spirit of God moving all in my soul.

It amazes me to think how God would take a sinner like me, dying in a world that is full of trouble, and on my way to a burning hell. Jesus Christ, God's own Son who was sitting high and looking low saw me after I had fallen down and could not get up. My wife didn't want me anymore, and there were so many others who had decided that they no longer had any use for me. Some people were saying that I was down and out for the count. Others said I was never going to amount to anything, but this same God my mother had told me about so many times when she was in trouble and didn't know what to do or how to do it, had a plan for me.

My mother would go into her secret closet and fall down on her knees crying out to the Lord. He would always show up and bring her through. I came to realize one day that God took the blinders off my eyes and allowed me to see this great God that my mother had always called on. I began to give God thanks for saving a sinner like me. It was then that I began to understand why I could not find the light at the end of the tunnel. I came to know and find the true light, and the true light shines in the hearts of men and women who love God. Jesus said in the book of **John 9:5** – *"As long as I am in the world, I am the light of the world."*

When folks had written me off and said I wouldn't amount to anything, what they did not know is that God had a plan and I was on his mind. **Psalms 115:12** reads, *"The Lord hath been mindful of us: He will bless us; He will bless the house of Israel; He will bless the house of Aaron."* I believe in what the Lord said. He is mindful, not just of me, but all of us.

I'm so glad that I learned not to always listen to what folks had to say because most folks have opinions, but God has the answer. I was reading in the word what the Bible has to say about opinions. You will find these words recorded in the Book of **1**

Kings 18:21 - *"And Elijah came unto all the people and said, how long halt ye between two opinions? If the Lord be God follow him: but if Baal, then follow him. And the people answered him not a word."*

I don't concern myself with folks' opinions because I know that everyone has one, and not everyone has Christ in their lives. Some folks preach circumstances and situations, but the Apostle Paul said in the first Book of **First Corinthians 1:23** – *"But we preach Christ crucified unto the Jews a stumbling block and unto the Greeks foolishness."*

Chapter 17

A NEW CREATURE IN CHRIST

Who knows why God has bought Pastor Howard to the kingdom for such a time as this. One thing I do know is that God knew that Pastor Howard would *cry loud, spare not, lift up his voice like a trumpet* (Isaiah 58), and tell a dying world that Jesus lives.

The gospel according to **Luke 15:10** says – *"Likewise I say unto you there is joy in the presence of the angels of God over one sinner that repented."* If I am just able to point just one soul to the cross then I will know that my living is not in vain.

We as people have the tendency to always try to hide something. Sometimes we try to hide our keys or money, even as a young man I remember how we used to play a game called "Hide and Go Seek." Truly I found out that we cannot hide anything from God! He is the all seeing God, the all knowing God, the all loving God and the all forgiving God.

I could not close this book without reminding all those folks who said I would be nothing and nobody, that without Christ in your life no matter who you are you're just a nobody that needs to know somebody who can save anybody. The Bible lets us know in the Book of **Romans 2:11** that *there is no respect of persons with God.* Let me stress that fact to those who use the words so easily that folks will turn out to be nothing.

I hope and pray that any parents out there still telling their children that they will amount to nothing would stop saying those words, because nobody knows what the end is going to be except God. I pray that you will take the time to read about how that God has the love and the power to take nothing and make something out of it. According to **Job 26:7** – *"He stretcheth out the north over the empty place and hangeth the earth upon nothing."*

I experienced a personal tragedy while writing the close of this book. On March 8, 2014, I received some very bad news concerning my friend. Their family home in Jersey City, New Jersey suffered a serious explosion. My friend and spiritual father in the gospel, Bishop William

Pickett, his lovely wife who I called mother, and two of their sons perished in the resulting fire. But the one thing that I do know is that they were truly, godly people. I don't have to wonder where they are. They were together in life, in death, and now in heaven.

I could never put my whole life story in one book, but I truly thank God for allowing me to be a testimony and a witness to lost souls. Jesus Christ, God's own Son, came into the world to let us know that we may never find a light in the tunnel, but if we can find Jesus then we can say of a truth that we have found the light of the world. When we find that light, the Bible says in **St. Matthew 5:16** – *"Let your light so shine before men that they may see your good works, and glorify your father which is in heaven."* I am so glad that God let me know in the Book of **1 Peter 2:9** – that he had called me out of darkness.

I can truly say today that I am a new creature in Christ. The Apostle Paul said in **1 Corinthians 15:31** – *"I die daily."* I no longer think the way I used to think. I don't walk the way I used to walk, nor do I talk the way I used to talk. Also like Paul I can truly say that I am crucified with Christ. You will find in **Galatians 2:20** – *"I am crucified with Christ: nevertheless I live; yet not I, but Christ liveth in me: and the life which I now live in the* *flesh I live by the faith of the Son of God, who loved me, and gave himself for me."*

The gospel according to **Mark 13:31** says - *"Heaven and earth shall pass away but the word of God shall stand."* I'm so glad now that I have something in my life that I can stand on and that is the word of God. I'm so grateful that God enabled me through all of my mess and madness. He looked down from his holy mountain and decided that He could trust me by putting me in the ministry.

Chapter 18

PERSONAL TESTIMONY

As I mentioned earlier, my family wasn't happy with my decision to become a pimp. Although my sister Laura was supportive of my desire to write this book, the actual process was a bit uncomfortable for her. She was uneasy with the world being introduced to "Pimping Al" and learning about my past life, after all, I am the Pastor of a church.

The book is finished, and it is my hope that Laura now understands that writing it was something I needed to do, not just for my son, or myself, but for anyone out there trying to make their way out of a dark situation. My goal has always been to share with others the fact that whatever your past – you can change and become new.

God always leaves a witness. What better person to provide this Personal Testimony than my sister, Evangelist Laura Frances Burris. She knew me as a boy. She knew me before I became a man. Laura knew me before I became "Pimping Al," and she witnessed my transformation into the person I am today, Pastor Albert Howard, Sr. She is someone who has known me most of my life, someone who prayed for me when I didn't know how to pray.

I'm so grateful that God changed my sister's life a long time ago. She is excited about what God has done for her brother. The book of **Job 16:19** reads, *"Also now behold my witness is in heaven and my record is on high."* My sister is a witness to where God has brought me from, and a witness to what God can do. I'm so grateful to have a sister who loves me so much until she refused to give up on me. She prayed night and day that God would not allow the devil to take my life. I'm grateful that God has allowed her to live long enough to see that the power is all in His hands. That power stopped her brother from pimping and gave him a new life as a Pastor . . .

Laura's Testimony

"My brothers and I grew up with a loving mother and father who always taught us to love one another and give to one another. My brother Albert was always the big boy of the family and was always there to have Thanksgiving, Christmas and New Year's dinner with us. I give God thanks, praise, honor and glory for my brother. Back in the day, we all thought he was really doing great, but one day I found out that the lord is greater than any "lifestyle" you could ever live, and when you find that God, it makes a difference.

One day we learned that Albert had become very sick. We found out he had a blockage in his lungs. If he had lain down that night the devil would have taken him out, but the prayers of the righteous availeth much. We didn't know at that time that he could have died, but God knew. We began to cry out for his soul and ask God to have mercy on him. My brother opened up his eyes, drugged out, all high and didn't know whether he was coming or going. He had a mother and father who were praying for him in the midst of death's situation. God stepped in even when my brother didn't know God, and kept his hands on him.

Today I can truly say it took my mother's death for my brother to seek God for himself. It took my mother going on to be with Jesus for Albert to understand that without Christ there is no life. All the cars, money and women, and all the drugs were failure because the devil had him duped up for death, but God came so that he could have life and have it more abundantly.

Albert has always been my big brother. He would fight at the drop of a hat. My baby brother and I were never fighters so we'd run to the one who knew how to fight. God fights our battles now. We no longer have to go to my big brother. I've got someone bigger than my brother. I've got a God who protects me, watches over me, and keeps me, so now our fellowship is sweet. I'm talking about the same God who raised me up when I didn't know who He was, kept me from death's door and told me that I love you with an everlasting love.

So many people are looking for love in all the wrong places, but God has the answer for love. **John 3:16** says *"For God so loved the world, that he gave his only* *begotten Son, that whosoever believeth in him should not perish, but have everlasting life."* The life of God is far greater than your diamonds and your rubies. Seek ye first the kingdom of God and all his righteousness will be added unto you. God is a God of addition, he doesn't subtract, He doesn't steal from you, He just wants you to come to him just as you are. He doesn't ask you to try and fix it because you don't know how to fix it, but God is a fixer. He's a heart regulator, a mind regulator and He will put you in his arms and take you places you could never go.

I thank God that He has raised my brother up with a better understanding. My brother always gave, back in the day when he didn't know God, and he's giving now. There's a reward for those that diligently seek out the lord and give.

I thank God for my Pastor years ago who saw God in my brother. He didn't put him down or make a mockery of him. He would tell him, "Albert, you need the lord." He didn't tell him about his lifestyle, he told him about Jesus style and Jesus style makes the difference. If you don't know Jesus style you don't have a life. Outside of Christ you'll run into a brick wall looking for something and you'll never ever be satisfied, nor happy.

Thank God for my nephew, Leonard. I want him to come back home and know that God is real. Sometimes we get off the beaten path and don't know God is real, but if you stay with God you'll never fail, you'll never lose, and the prize is far greater than anything you think you want in life. I say to all those who read this book, find Jesus. He's the answer. God bless you. Love you with the love of the lord."

Chapter 19

FORGIVENESS

In closing, I would like to ask of God and all of my children, forgiveness. I pray that my children will forgive me for what I have put them through in living bad examples in their lives. To my children who were raised in the home on Larose Avenue in Cleveland, Ohio; Dwight Howard, Leonard Howard, Sereta Howard and Albert Howard, Jr., and also to my children who were raised in the home on Hobert Avenue in Plainfield, New Jersey; Alana Bland, Elijah Bland, Demetrius Stephens, Mikal Jones, Jaquetta Carver, and Julia Moore who was raised in my home earlier with Lynda Stephens, I apologize.

Almetra Hodges was not raised in my home and we did not share a close father-daughter relationship. Maybe that was a blessing in disguise for her.

I thank God that most of my children have grown past my pimping years, and are seeing and spending time with this father who is now setting a better example as a Pastor and man of God. My prayer is that God will cover them all under the precious blood of his Son Jesus, who came to seek and save those that are lost. **Luke 19:10.**

The Bible says in **Romans 13:7** – *"Render therefore to all their dues: tribute to whom tribute is due; custom to whom custom; fear to whom fear; honor to whom honor."* I would like to take this time to give honor to my son, Leonard Howard, known as Lenbob Howard. The Bible says to give honor where honor is due, and I know in my heart that my son Leonard deserves honor, because had it not been for his inspiring me to write this book it would not have been so.

Leonard has been incarcerated for 20+ years and while there he himself has become a writer. Leonard has authored two books: "The Son of a Pimp" and "The Son of a Pimp, Part II" based on true stories. My prayer is that God will always keep Leonard Howard covered under the precious blood of his Son Jesus.

I'm so grateful and thankful because I had no mind of telling this story at all, but Leonard encouraged me. It is not for fortune or fame, but truly for the lost souls that are in the world today.

My journey has been amazing and I have been blessed through it all. I'm thankful for God's mercy and grace for He truly had a plan for my life. Throughout my 30 plus years as "Pimping Al," God knew that I would be changed, renewed and transformed to be a blessing to his people.

To God be the glory.

❧ SPECIAL THANKS ☙

I'd like to give special thanks to Belinda Diane Jones, Colleen Carpenter - Word Processing Diva.com (Book Consultant, Typist & Proofreader), Mary Bland, Lynda Stephens, my son, Leonard Howard and all of you who have helped to make this book possible.

God has brought me from a mighty long way...

Psalm 40:2

He brought me up also out of an horrible pit, out of the miry clay, and set my feet upon a rock, and established my goings.